The Essential
Guide to
Drawing

The Essential
Guide to
Drawing

Barrington Barber

ARCTURUS

This edition published in 2021 by Arcturus Publishing Limited
26/27 Bickels Yard, 151–153 Bermondsey Street,
London SE1 3HA

ISBN: 978-1-3988-0373-2
AD008595UK

Printed in China

CONTENTS

Introduction

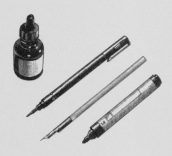

Learning to draw is not difficult – everybody learns to walk, talk, read and write at an early age, and discovering how to draw is easier than any of those processes! Drawing is merely making marks on paper which represent some visual experience. All it takes to draw effectively is the desire to do it, a little persistence, the ability to observe and a willingness to take time to correct any mistakes. This last point is very important as mistakes are not in themselves bad – they are opportunities for improvement, as long as you always put them right so that you will know what to do the next time.

Many of the exercises in this book incorporate the time-honoured methods practised by art students and professional artists. If these are followed diligently, they should bring about marked progress in your drawing skills. With consistent practice and regular repetition of the exercises, you should be able to draw competently and from there you will see your skills burgeon. Don't be put off by difficulties along the way, because they can be overcome with determination and a lot of practice and this means you are actively learning, even if it may seem a bit of a struggle at times. The main thing is to practise regularly and keep correcting your mistakes as you see them. Try not to become impatient with yourself, as the time you spend altering your drawings to improve them is time well spent.

Work with other students as often as you can, because this also helps your progress. Drawing may seem like a private exercise, but in fact it's a public one, because your drawings are for others to see and appreciate. Show your work to other people and listen to what they say; don't just accept or reject their praise or criticism, but check up on your work to see if they have seen something you haven't. If other people's views aren't very complimentary, don't take offence. Neither praise nor criticism matters except in so far as it helps you to see your work more objectively. Although at first a more experienced artist's views are of great value, eventually you have to become your own toughest critic, assessing exactly how a drawing has succeeded and how it has not worked.

Talk to professional artists about their work if you get the chance. Go to art shows and galleries to see what the 'competition' is like, be it from the old masters or your contemporaries. All this experience will help you to move your work in the right direction. Although working through this book will help you along your path to drawing well, it is up to you to notice your weaknesses and strengths, trying to correct the former and building on the latter.

Steady, hard work can accomplish more than talent by itself, so don't give up when you are feeling discouraged; drawing is a marvellously satisfying activity, even if you never get your work into a gallery. Enjoy yourself!

Barrington Barber

Chapter One

MARKS AND MATERIALS

When you first begin to draw, it can be hard to know just what you should do to set off on the right track, so in this chapter we shall look at what drawing is about at the most basic level. Put simply, it's making marks on paper, and initially any marks will do.

We shall look first at how to handle your equipment and adopt a good drawing position. Then I'll show you the materials that you can draw with, giving you some choices so that you'll have fun and explore different possibilities. The most obvious tool to use when you are starting out is pencil, as you will have used these since you were a child and will feel very comfortable with them. But I encourage you to try a variety of mediums to see the different marks they make, enjoying the way you can expand your range of techniques.

Don't worry if at first you make rather a mess of the exercises; no one ever became any good at art without making lots of mistakes to start with. Experimentation is the way that art evolves; it is not just the preserve of scientists.

Holding the Tools

Holding your pencil, pen, brush or chalk doesn't always have to be the same as you would hold a fountain pen. Sometimes you get better, freer results by holding them as you would hold a stick or a house-painting brush. The only one that you will have to hold the same way as a fountain pen is the dip pen with ink because it is very difficult to manipulate any other way. We show here the variety of ways of holding these implements. You may need to practise these different ways to become good at them.

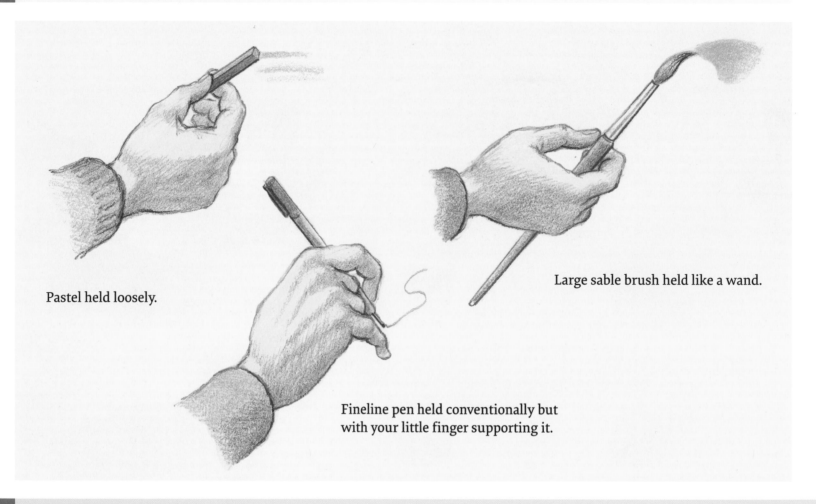

Pastel held loosely.

Large sable brush held like a wand.

Fineline pen held conventionally but with your little finger supporting it.

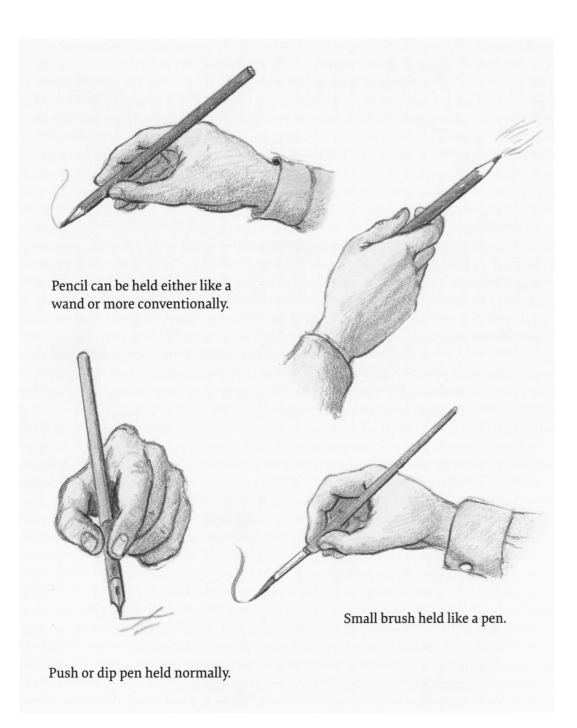

Pencil can be held either like a wand or more conventionally.

Push or dip pen held normally.

Small brush held like a pen.

Drawing Positions

In order to draw well, make sure that you are comfortably positioned – try different positions to find the one most suited to you. It is nearly always best to have your drawing supported on a sloping board. This is particularly useful when using watercolours because it allows the water to run down the paper and makes it easier to control the intensity of your colour.

For most drawing, except with pen and ink, I prefer to stand up using an easel, but sometimes it is not convenient nor does it always give the best results. When working with pen and ink, you should keep your paper surface less upright, otherwise the ink does not flow properly to the nib, and the same is true to a certain extent with brushwork in watercolour. But having the paper absolutely flat is not a good idea because you tend to view it too much from one angle, which can give rise to distortion.

Standing at an easel.

Sitting down with the board supported by the back of another chair.

Drawing with pastels on a board propped up on a table.

Probably the best position for drawing in pen and ink.

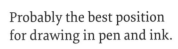

Standing up with a sketchpad

Pencil

The most common medium for drawing is pencil. Use B-grade pencils as they make a darker mark with less pressure required than the harder H pencils. Ideally you should have B, 2B, 4B, 6B and 8B as a range.

B-grade pencils are soft and wear down quite fast, so have several sharp pencils to hand. It will interrupt the flow of your work if you have to keep stopping to sharpen your pencil.

1. When you're ready, start drawing a wavy line in any direction just to get the feel of the pencil on the paper. This is more important than it may seem, because experiencing through your hand the way the pencil meets the paper gives your drawing greater sensitivity.

2. Scribble lines in all directions to make a patch of dark tone.

3. Then try a series of quickly made lines, all in the same direction and as close together as you can, to make a patch of tone.

4. Next, draw a number of lines in all directions, but shorter and spaced around to build up like a layer of twigs.

5. Draw a tonal patch with all the lines going in one direction in vertical strokes.

6. Next, draw horizontal strokes in the same manner.

7. Now combine horizontal and vertical lines with diagonals to produce a very dark patch of tone.

8. Draw a circle as accurately as you can. Although it's easy enough to imagine a perfect circle, drawing one takes careful work and yours will probably look like the one shown.

9. Now add a bit of tone to one side of your circle to give the impression of a three-dimensional sphere. Put a patch of tone underneath the sphere, to look like a shadow.

10. Now try a drawing of a group of leaves, keeping it simple and just aiming to express the feel of the plant's growth.

11. Similarly, draw a flower shape – don't try to be too exact at this stage.

Now we are taking a further step towards picture-making, because you are going to attempt a shape that resembles something that you might want to draw.

12. First draw a diamond shape that is flatter horizontally than vertically.

13. Then draw three vertical lines down from the left corner, the lower centre corner and the right corner. All the lines should be parallel to each other and about the same length, so that the central one ends a little lower.

14. Now draw lines from the lower ends of the verticals, similar to the lower sides of the original diamond shape. This now looks like a cube shape.

15. To increase the illusion of three dimensions, make a light tone across the background space to about halfway down the cube, then put tone over the two lower surfaces of the cube. Make the tone on one of the lower sides even darker. To finish off the illusion, draw a tone from the bottom of the darkest side of the cube across the surface that the cube is standing on. The final result looks like a box standing on a surface.

Pen and Ink

To draw with pen and ink, the most obvious tool to go for is a graphic pen. These are available in several sizes, and you will need a 0.1, a 0.3 and a 0.8 to give you a fine line and two rather thicker lines. You can buy them in any stationery or art supplies shop. There's no variation in the line from these pens, so if this is what you want, use instead a push pen with a fine nib and a bottle of black Indian ink. If the pen nib is flexible enough you can vary the thickness of the line at will, by exerting or releasing a little more pressure on the pen. These pens are available from a good art shop or a specialist pen shop.

1. To start with, try out your pen by drawing a wavering line that winds around and back over itself.

2. Now, as with the pencil, make a fairly rough scribbled area as shown – don't worry about the direction or length of the lines drawn.

3. This time make your lines more deliberate, all in the same direction and as close together as you can without them touching.

4. Now have a go at short marks that go in all directions and overlay each other. Keep the texture as even as you can so that there are no obvious gaps showing.

5. The next stage is to draw patches of tone with the pen as I have shown in the examples, first diagonally, then vertically and horizontally.

6. Then draw all the lines in four directions, overlaying them to build up a texture that can be read as a tone.

7. Next, draw a circle in ink, in the same way as you did with your pencil.

8. Now, using textured marks, as in the example, try to make a convincing sphere shape out of your circle.

9. Now draw a spray of leaves. Because the pen is so much more definite than the pencil you will have to draw lightly and finely, or else the lines will become too clumsy.

10. Then draw a flower head on a stalk. Treat your drawing loosely, as if using a pencil, and the marks will look attractive.

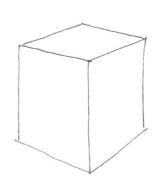

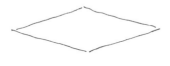
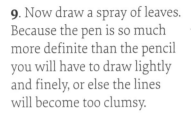

11. Now have a go at drawing the same cube shape as before, but this time in ink. Note how in the last stage the lines are quite carefully drawn in one direction and then overlaid with other lines in contrary directions to build up the tone.

Charcoal and Conté

These mediums are favoured by many artists as they give a quick result in terms of tone and flexibility. Charcoal comes in sticks of varying thickness, of which you will only need about two. It is very brittle and breaks easily, so you really have to use a light touch; it always makes a dark mark so you don't need to press at all. For something stronger and less easily smudged, try conté sticks, made of powdered graphite or charcoal compressed with a binder. Either way you will need to buy some fixative to spray your drawings with to make sure that they don't smudge; do this outdoors if possible as the fumes can be unpleasant.

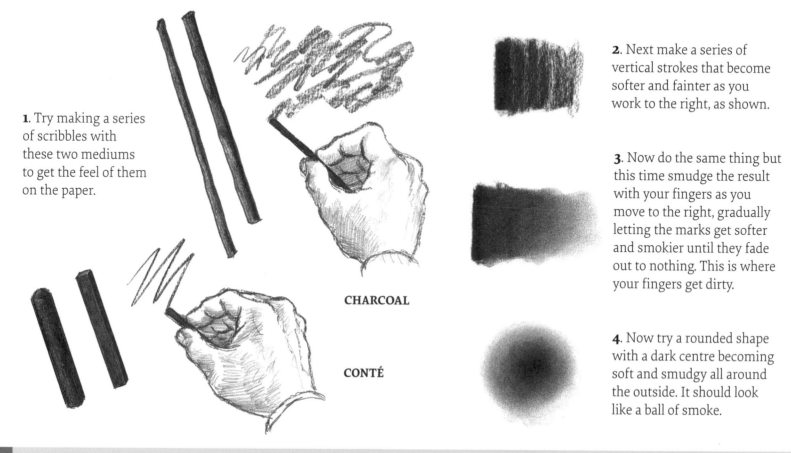

1. Try making a series of scribbles with these two mediums to get the feel of them on the paper.

CHARCOAL

CONTÉ

2. Next make a series of vertical strokes that become softer and fainter as you work to the right, as shown.

3. Now do the same thing but this time smudge the result with your fingers as you move to the right, gradually letting the marks get softer and smokier until they fade out to nothing. This is where your fingers get dirty.

4. Now try a rounded shape with a dark centre becoming soft and smudgy all around the outside. It should look like a ball of smoke.

Now go through a similar set of exercises with the charcoal or conté stick, but this time using slightly different marks. Finger smudging helps you to give a softer edge to the tones.

5. First, create a scribble that gets darker and darker, overlapping the marks to give more density.

6. Next, make a series of scribbly lines to produce a much lighter tone. Keep your touch on the paper quite soft, with no pressure.

7. Now make a series of dark lines then smudge them until you have something that looks like a dark cloud with no defined edges.

9. Next try a cube. Build up the tone on two sides, being careful to leave the top surface white. Use your finger to create a smudged shadow to the front of the cube.

8. Now draw a circle. Draw in the areas of shadow, leaving a white highlight to give the sphere volume. Your circles will be getting better as you've done a few now!

10. Finally, make some quick drawings of leaves and a flower, smudging parts with your finger to give some hint of shadows or texture.

Brush and Wash

This form of drawing uses a brush instead of a pencil and is a useful technique. I recommend two watercolour brushes of different sizes, and some dark watercolour paint or soluble ink. Buy round brushes, which come to a point when they are wet – the best type for this are those made of sable hair. Watercolour paper is the ideal surface, but if you prefer to use cheaper cartridge paper you should buy a fairly heavy one or the water will make it cockle.

Using brushes of radically different sizes gives you plenty of choice for mark-making.

3. Now try a darker tone, gradually making it lighter as you progress to the right by adding more water for each stroke.

1. Start by making gentle swashes of lines with each of the brushes to get the feel of how they work.

4. Now, with the smaller brush, swish a few lines of tone without taking the brush off the paper.

5. Starting with a very dark tone, dilute it down as you move to the right until it seems to disappear into nothing. Ideally you should be able to go from the very darkest tone to almost white by this method, but don't worry if at first you can't achieve it – more practice will improve your efforts.

2. Then make a patch of tone – quite a light one.

6. Now try painting a few leaf-shapes like the ones you did with your dry mediums, only this time it will be much easier to get the shape in one stroke. When it is dry, paint in a few darker lines to show the veins on the leaves.

7. Now repeat the same procedure with a flower shape.

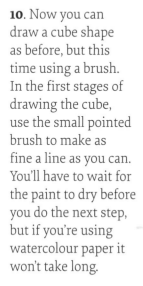

8. Again try to draw a perfect circle.

9. With another circle, put in some tone over the lower three-quarters of the shape, using a wet brush to fade out the tone near the top of the sphere. Place a cast shadow beneath the sphere, fading it off towards the outer edge.

10. Now you can draw a cube shape as before, but this time using a brush. In the first stages of drawing the cube, use the small pointed brush to make as fine a line as you can. You'll have to wait for the paint to dry before you do the next step, but if you're using watercolour paper it won't take long.

11. Paint a wash as carefully as you can with your large brush, giving a tonal background halfway down the cube and covering the two lower sides in the same tone. Also put in a cast shadow, washing it away to nothing at the far end of the shadow.

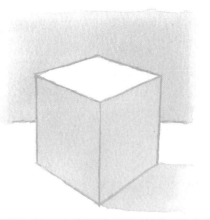

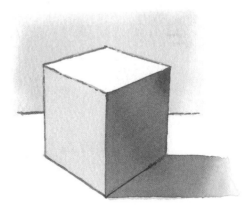

12. Now just darken one side and the adjacent shadow to complete the picture. You may want to strengthen the lines a little around the cube as I did to make it more positive.

The Colour Wheel

When it comes to drawing in colour, it can be useful to have an understanding of colour theory – that is, how different colours relate to each other and can be mixed together. The simple device of the colour wheel is very useful for demonstrating the relationships between the different colours of the spectrum and holds true for any of the mediums you will be using.

The diagram opposite shows an inner circle of colour containing the three primaries, red, yellow and blue (see also swatch below). 'Primary' means you cannot break these colours down into any components. They are the three basic colours from which all others are made.

The colours made by mixing two primary colours together are called secondary colours, and these are annotated on the outer ring of the colour wheel. Blue mixed with red makes purple; red mixed with yellow makes orange; and yellow mixed with blue makes green.

The tertiary colours, also indicated on the colour wheel, are mixtures of the primary colours with the secondary colours. By mixing primary and secondary colours together, you can make a complete spectrum with all the colours you need.

Now have a look at the colours that are opposite one another. They 'complement' each other as they render the greatest contrast between themselves and, as a result, have the most impact when placed together in, for example, a picture. Examples of complementary colour pairs are: red and green; blue and orange; yellow and purple.

Browns, also known as neutral colours, do not appear on the colour wheel but are made by mixing together complementary colours in varying amounts.

You can vary the tint of any colour by adding white to lighten it. You can deepen the shade of any colour by adding black to darken it, or you can tone it down by adding grey.

Of course different colour mediums create varying effects and you will have to experiment to become familiar with them, but these basic colour facts hold true.

The primary colours

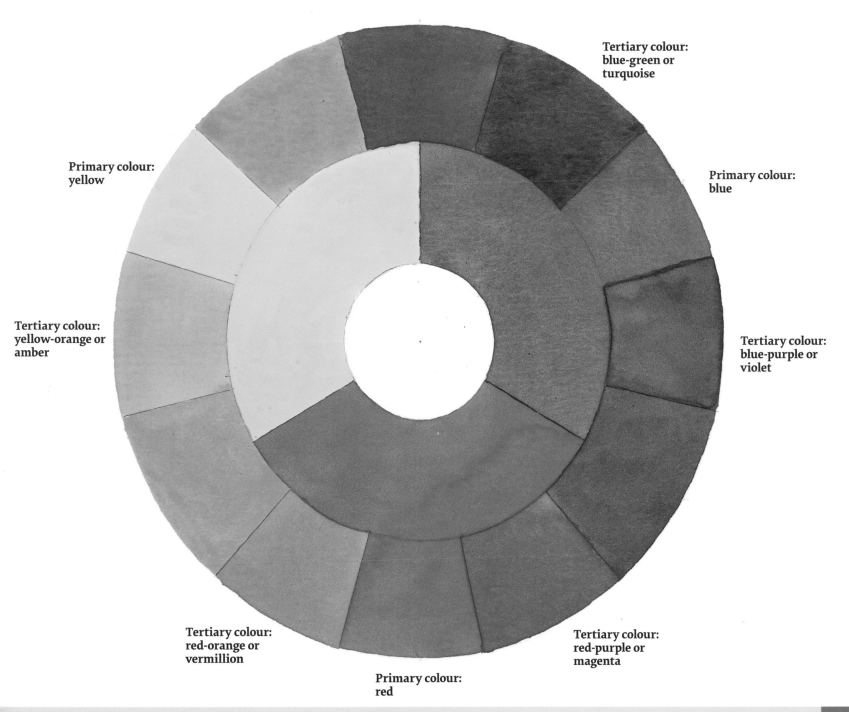

Tertiary colour: blue-green or turquoise

Primary colour: yellow

Primary colour: blue

Tertiary colour: yellow-orange or amber

Tertiary colour: blue-purple or violet

Tertiary colour: red-orange or vermillion

Tertiary colour: red-purple or magenta

Primary colour: red

Coloured Pencil

Coloured pencils are one form of colour that almost everybody has had some experience of using, from quite an early age. You will need a good range of colours, and different brands produce slightly different ranges, so sometimes a mix of brands can be to your advantage. Make sure all your pencils are well sharpened before you start, because you get a better texture for the colour intensity if you do.

1. To start with, give yourself an idea of the relative colour power of the different pencils by making a chart, drawing a patch of colour, as shown, as strongly as you can without breaking the lead. As you will see, there is a limitation on the intensity of these colours compared with paints or pastels. This means that when you are drawing pictures in this medium you will be producing a rather soft and gentle colour impact. The best results will be from careful and delicate drawing.

2. Having made your chart, next try drawing with fairly gentle strokes all in one direction, like shading with an ordinary pencil. Keep the strokes as close together as you can in order to produce a uniform effect.

3. Then make a series of short marks in various directions, producing an overall texture that looks a bit like wood. I've used brown here.

4. Now try different ways of covering a surface, as shown; first a wandering line which doubles back on itself to produce a sort of scribble area. I've used green, but try several colours yourself.

5. The next series of marks are almost dots and you can decide whether you prefer a scattering of dots or very short marks. Cover the area as uniformly as you can.

6. Then try the exercise of taking closely marked straight lines alongside and across each other to build up a rather denser texture.

7. Now you can attempt overlaying one colour with another. To keep it simple, I have just done strokes all in one direction for the first colour and in a contrary direction for the second. My combinations are yellow-green then green, green then brown, yellow then red, and yellow then blue. But any combination is worth trying, so do experiment.

8. Finally, practise controlling your pencil by starting with a hard stroke that softens off. Then select another colour; its complementary contrast (the pairs of colours that lie opposite each other on the colour wheel – see pages 23–4) would be best. Start off gently with this one before making the stroke, and colour, stronger towards the end.

Coloured Ink

Fineline fibre-tipped pens in a range of colours represent coloured ink in its simplest commercial form. You can buy them separately or in packs of a complete colour range. The other option is to use a fine dip pen and nib and bottles of either coloured Indian ink or concentrated liquid watercolours that also come in bottles. These work just as well as fibre-tips and last much longer.

1. The first task is to test their effect by scribbling a patch of colour with each individual pen. Lay them alongside each other to see how they contrast or harmonize. With this type of ink, the colours are usually quite sharp and strong so that the only problem is how to soften them and combine them.

2. One way of pulling two colours together is by making very small marks of colour starting heavily on the left and gradually dispersing them more widely as you move to the right. Then do the same thing with another colour from the right towards the left. If one colour is a lot stronger or darker than the other you may have to fade it out more quickly. In my examples, I've done from yellow to orange and from red to green. In the latter, note that the light green was helped a bit towards its stronger end by another deeper green.

3. Next, try overlaying strokes of two different colours with the strokes of one colour opposed by strokes of another at almost right angles over the top. I show blue over green, dark blue over pink, light brown over grey and dark brown over red.

4. In order to get a gentler variety of tone in your colour, do the outlines in ink and then use another medium to produce areas of tone within the shapes. I have used coloured pencils inside the square outline of ink. This can work quite well.

5. Lastly, I show a set of marks made by thicker felt-tipped markers which, as you can see, will strengthen any colours where you feel you need a more powerful emphasis.

Coloured Pastels and Chalk

The most expressive way of drawing in colour, as opposed to painting, is by using artists' pastels or chalk, which are made of the same pigments as paints, but held in the form of a stick. Most artists will use both the hard and the soft variety of pastel, depending on the effects they are after, but if you are an absolute beginner at this medium, the hard pastels are easier to start with. They are often also called conté crayons.

1. When using pastels or conté crayons, work on tinted stock such as Ingres paper, testing your colours by selecting a creamy-beige toned paper and a darker brown-grey (opposite). On the lighter paper, first make a sort of chart with one stroke of each colour using the thickness of the pastel. This will give you some idea of the density of tone and brightness of colour for each crayon.

2. Now make a patch of colour, scribbling chalk back and forth over a small area. Then with your finger or thumb, smudge about half of it along the bottom section to see what happens when the colour is worked over. You will not need to treat every colour like this, but do enough to give you an idea of how it looks.

3. Next, make an overall scribble of tone starting lightly and getting heavier and heavier – without crushing the crayon – but getting the most solid colour value from each one. This will show how the colour can be varied in intensity.

4. Now have a go at doing the same thing on the darker of the two papers. Note how different colours stand out in different ways. A red that looks quite dark and strong on the beige paper looks vibrant and glowing on the dark brown. Notice how the dark tones look heavier on the light paper and more subdued on the dark paper. See how the tonal variation also applies to the smudging exercise. Smudging the colours allows you to produce a larger mass of smoother colour if you require it. Most artists tend to use a mid- to dark tone for working in this medium, but some eighteenth-century artists working on whitish paper produced pictures that looked, from a distance, like oil paintings.

This is a medium favoured by professional artists because it is like dry painting: easier to transport and with much the same possibilities as watercolours or oil paint. However, you will have to invest in a good spray-on fixative to hold loose particles of chalk and prevent your picture fading away. Some artists don't like fixing their work because it sometimes affects the colour values, especially when the pastel is overlaid thickly, one colour over another. Instead, they shake off the excess pastel by tapping it gently, and keep putting on and tapping off until they get the result that they desire. Nevertheless, to keep it safe, the work will have to be overlaid with a sheet of acid-free tissue paper or put immediately under framed glass.

Watercolour

Watercolour is the colour version of brush and wash that we looked at on pages 20–1. As with brush and wash, when you come to use watercolours, first familiarize yourself with the quality of the paint and its covering power. It is a very flexible medium and can produce brilliant results in the hands of a practised painter. But, even with a beginner, the results can sometimes be quite marvellous because, some of the time, you rely on what are called 'happy accidents'. That is when you get an interesting result even though you don't plan it.

1. Take a large soft brush (a size 7 sable would be ideal) and wet it, then take the strongest tone you can on your brush and lay strokes of each colour next to one another so that you get a clear idea of their relative power. Do this exercise on a piece of white watercolour paper for the best results. Thin paper will only cockle (go wavy).

2. Having made a patch for each colour in your paintbox, find out how the intensity can be reduced by adding water to it. Starting with a solid patch (I started with yellow), brush out from left to right, then add more and more water until the colour has almost faded to nothing. Try to do it as evenly as you can. You will improve with practice but, as you can see from my examples of yellow, red, blue, viridian, brown and purple, some have come out much patchier than others. However, this only shows that a patchy quality is sometimes quite acceptable.

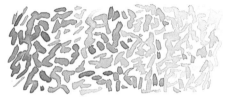

3. Get accustomed to the idea of drawing with the brush. As you can see from the next set of exercises, coloured shapes have been formed by pulling the tip of the brush across the paper with various twists and turns that are sometimes thicker and sometimes thinner. Try the same method with the brush, making short strokes and small blobs.

4. Using two colours, make downward strokes where each stroke floods into the next one, producing an all-over patch of colour. Try it with the strokes going up and down alternately.

5. Drag the loaded brush across the paper horizontally, allowing each stroke to flood into the one above. Do all this with your paper attached to a sloping board. This allows the water to run smoothly down the paper. Whatever you do, try to avoid the mistake of going back over the painted areas because this always produces patchy colour effects.

Having done all this, repeat the exercise with a smaller brush such as a size 2, which has a narrower point.

Chapter Two

FIRST STEPS IN DRAWING

Once you've become familiar with the marks that different drawing materials make you can really get going on drawing from life. To begin with, we shall concentrate on making line drawings of a series of ordinary household objects, learning to observe them in detail and draw them accurately. Then I will show how you can add some shading to give your drawings a sense of being solid objects.

We shall take an initial look at some of the subjects that are available for you to practise your drawing skills on. Man-made objects, the natural world and the human form offer an endless source of material, and most of us don't need to look far to find a subject to draw within these areas, all of which will be explored in more depth later in this book.

The exercises over the following pages should be fun, so try to feel at ease as you do them. Don't grip the pencil too tightly, keep your shoulders relaxed and don't hunch up or get too close to your work. Draw what interests you and don't worry about mistakes – just correct them when you see them.

Line Drawing

To start with we'll concentrate on the outline shapes of some familiar household objects. I have chosen some items from my own house – yours don't have to be exactly the same, but it will help you to follow my drawings as well as having the actual object in front of you.

Before you start, look very carefully at each object to familiarize yourself with its shape. I have used glass objects for the first exercises, because you can see through them to understand how the shape works.

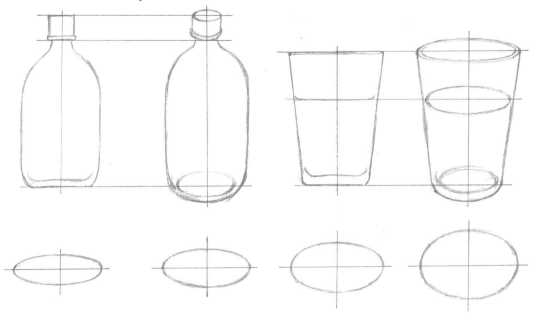

My first object is a bottle, seen directly from the side. As it was exactly symmetrical, I put in a central line first. Then I drew an outline of its shape including the screw top, making sure that both sides were symmetrical.

From a higher eye-level, I could see the bottle's rounded shape. To show this I needed to draw the elliptical shapes that circles make when seen from an oblique angle. Again I carefully constructed the shape either side of a central vertical line.

The ellipses shown below the bottles demonstrate how they become flattened to a greater or lesser degree depending upon the eye-level from which a rounded object is seen.

Although they become deeper across the vertical axis the further they are below your eye-level, the horizontal axis remains the same width. Don't be put off by the difficulty of drawing ellipses, because even professional artists don't find them so easy; with practice, you will be able to draw them well.

The next object is a glass tumbler with some water in it – slightly easier to draw than the bottle because it has straight sides. Draw the outline first at eye-level and then seen from slightly above. In the latter drawing there are three ellipses: the top edge of the glass, the surface of the water and the bottom of the glass.

The third object, a wine glass with some liquid in it, is a bit harder. Here you will see that there are three ellipses of varying width, but the object is still symmetrical from side to side. Go carefully and enjoy discovering the exact shape.

Next, some opaque subjects, starting with a bowl (below right). The side view drawing is easy enough; make the curve as accurate as you can, and then tackle the view from just above. This time you aren't able to see through the sides, so you have only one edge of the lower ellipse to draw.

The cup and saucer is more complex, but with a bit of steady care and attention you will soon get the shape right. Drawing it from above is a little harder and because you can't see through the porcelain it might be trickier to get the lower ellipses right first time.

The jug should be a bit easier after the cup and saucer, and it is placed here on purpose so that the effort you make on the more complex drawing pays off on the easier one. As before, draw the exact side view first before you depict it more naturally, seen from slightly above.

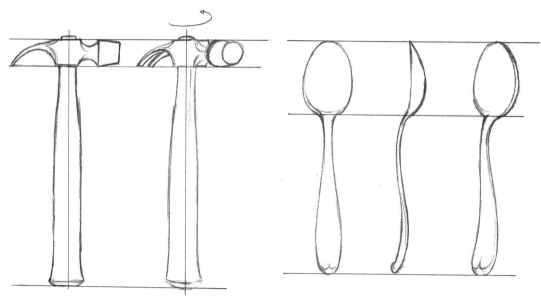

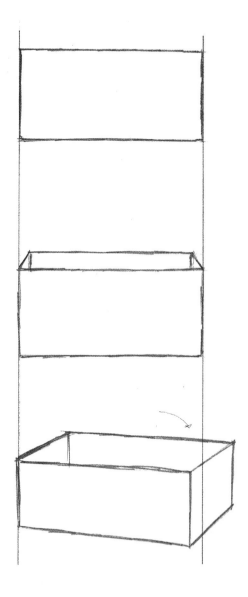

Now you're ready to move on to a series of objects which are of varying difficulty. The drawing of the hammer is quite easy from the exact side view but is a bit trickier from a more oblique view.

Three ways to draw the spoon are shown, from the exact front and from the exact side, as well as a more natural three-quarter view.

The pot is not too difficult if you have completed all the other objects so far, and the box is very simple – but beware of the third version, a slightly more complex view where the perspective can easily go wrong (see page 122 for how to construct two-point perspective when drawing buildings, a technique that can also be applied to smaller objects such as this box).

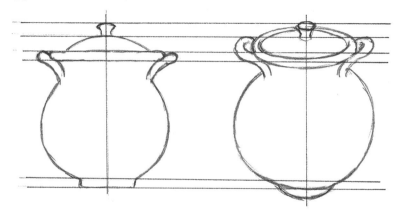

The saucepan and the teapot are of varying difficulty, but by now you are getting used to the problems of drawing like this. This sequence of objects is merely to give you practice in drawing, doing as many as you can in the time you have available.

Shading

So far we have concentrated on the outline shapes of objects. However to make them look more three-dimensional and substantial, the use of shading of some sort is needed. Here we look at how you can add shading in graphite pencil and in coloured pencil.

First, make line drawings of the objects as accurately as possible. On the book, use shading to show the curve of the spine, increasing the tone to a strong black line where the book meets the surface. I used fine lines to convey an effect of densely packed pages and a small cast shadow to anchor the book to the surface.

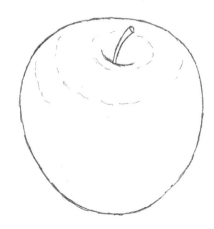

The apple needs to be shaded in a vertical direction between the upper surface and the bottom, concentrating on the left-hand side to indicate the direction of the light. Also add a cast shadow and shading where the apple stalk comes out of its hollow.

Shading using coloured pencils requires much the same technique as for graphite pencils. After you have drawn an outline of the main shapes, you can start to build up shading using your chosen colours. Here, I used the light ochre colour of the pot I was drawing, with smoothly hatched lines in the lightest areas graduating to a dark grey on the shaded side. This pot needs quite heavy tone in the interior space to give some idea of the inner hollow. I used blue in addition to dark grey for the shadowed areas, as this contrasted nicely with the ochre and lent interest to the drawing. Finally, I added a small cast shadow and a light blue background part-way up the pot, to increase the impression of a real pot sitting on a table surface.

More Complex Objects

Once you have gained some confidence at drawing simple objects around the house, choose some items with more complex shapes. Try drawing a single workshop tool, like this pair of pliers. Before you start, have a good look at them. Often, appreciating how something works helps your drawing of it.

Step 1

First, draw the main outline shape, taking your time as this is the most important stage in the drawing. Don't use a viewpoint immediately above the pliers, as you won't be able to produce a three-dimensional effect.

Step 2

When you are sure that the shape is right, block in very simply all the areas where you can see shading, using just one tone.

Step 3

Having put in the shading with one tone, you can now add darker tones to emphasize the dimensions and the materiality.

Step 1

Next, something even more complicated, like this pair of binoculars. Start with the main shape, making sure you get all the parts the correct size in relation to all the others.

Step 2

Again, block in the shadow using the lightest tone. Now work up the darker tones, until your drawing starts to look more like the shape and material of the original. Watch out for any reflections, which you should leave white.

Negative Space

This next object is larger and more difficult. It is a child's chair, viewed from an angle that reveals the spaces between the rungs and the back of the chair. These spaces between and around objects are called 'negative spaces' (or sometimes 'negative shapes') and observing them will help you to draw more accurately.

Step 1

Drawing the first outline is in some ways easier than with a more solid object, because it is quite clear how the chair is constructed. Keep the drawing loose and open to start with, so that you can link the legs and rungs across the main structure.

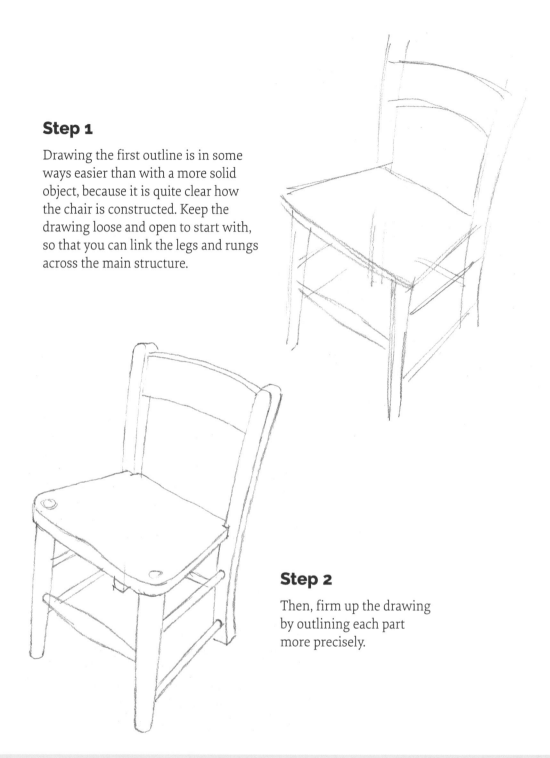

Step 2

Then, firm up the drawing by outlining each part more precisely.

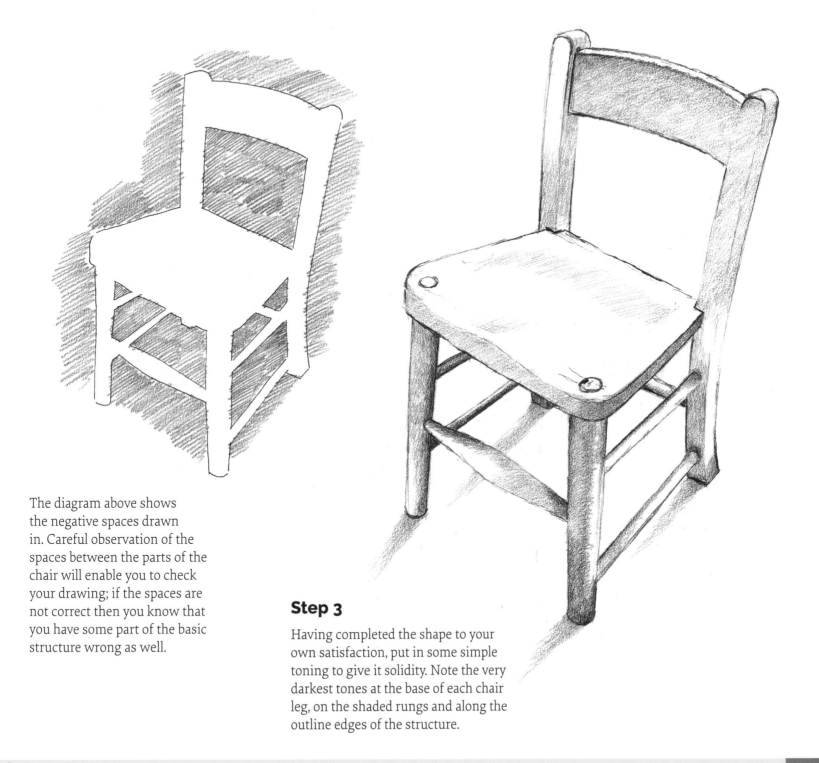

The diagram above shows the negative spaces drawn in. Careful observation of the spaces between the parts of the chair will enable you to check your drawing; if the spaces are not correct then you know that you have some part of the basic structure wrong as well.

Step 3

Having completed the shape to your own satisfaction, put in some simple toning to give it solidity. Note the very darkest tones at the base of each chair leg, on the shaded rungs and along the outline edges of the structure.

Large Objects

You have practised drawing small objects such as cups and cutlery to give you the idea of showing man-made forms, as well as a little chair – now it is time to tackle a much larger object. Although it is not a bulky item, a bicycle is quite complex and you will need to study how its various shapes fit together.

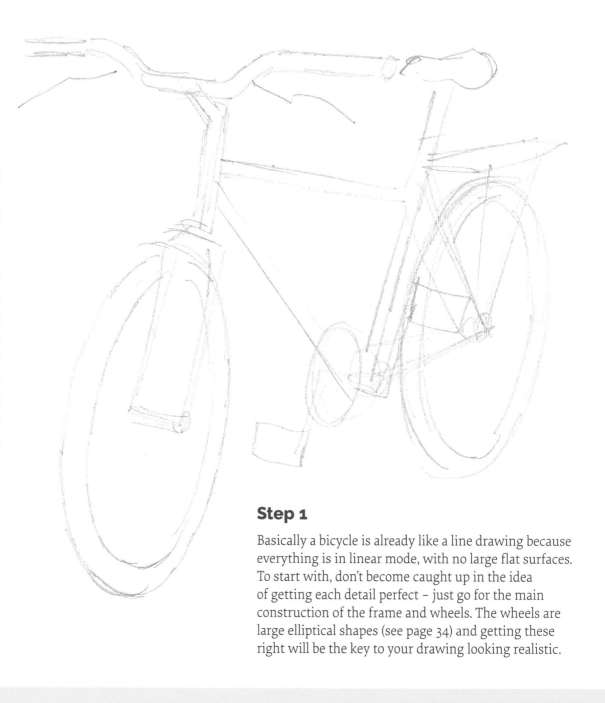

Step 1

Basically a bicycle is already like a line drawing because everything is in linear mode, with no large flat surfaces. To start with, don't become caught up in the idea of getting each detail perfect – just go for the main construction of the frame and wheels. The wheels are large elliptical shapes (see page 34) and getting these right will be the key to your drawing looking realistic.

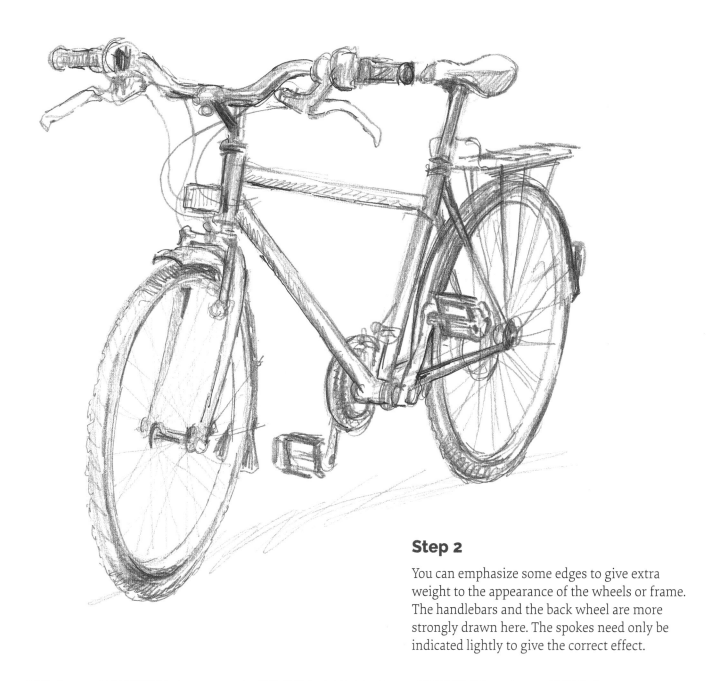

Step 2

You can emphasize some edges to give extra weight to the appearance of the wheels or frame. The handlebars and the back wheel are more strongly drawn here. The spokes need only be indicated lightly to give the correct effect.

Plants

All of the objects we have studied so far have been man-made, composed of largely geometric forms and smooth surfaces. The natural world also offers an endless source of drawing material and here we look at some of the subtle and delicate shapes of leaves and flowers. Start with simple forms that you feel comfortable with.

I have started here with a small four-petalled blossom using a soft conté pencil, which leaves a rather chalky line. I've drawn in the parts in shadow, but kept it all fairly simple.

The next subject I drew was this stalk with leaves. I didn't try to show texture, satisfying myself with the shapes of the leaves and their arrangement on the stalk, with the main veins drawn in as well. Try this, looking only at the outline shape of your plant, but drawing every detail of the edges.

Flowers make excellent subjects for practising your drawing skills upon because they can easily be picked out from the background vegetation and have quite complex shapes.

These rose and clematis flowers present interesting shapes and need to be carefully studied in order to get the feel of their delicate forms. At this stage, just concentrate on getting the shape right; later, when you're more expert, you'll want to achieve a more sensitive rendition.

By contrast with the examples on the previous page, this lily is a very sculptural-looking flower. It is shown in three stages of bloom; as it is just opening, almost fully extended, and at full bloom just before it begins to die off.

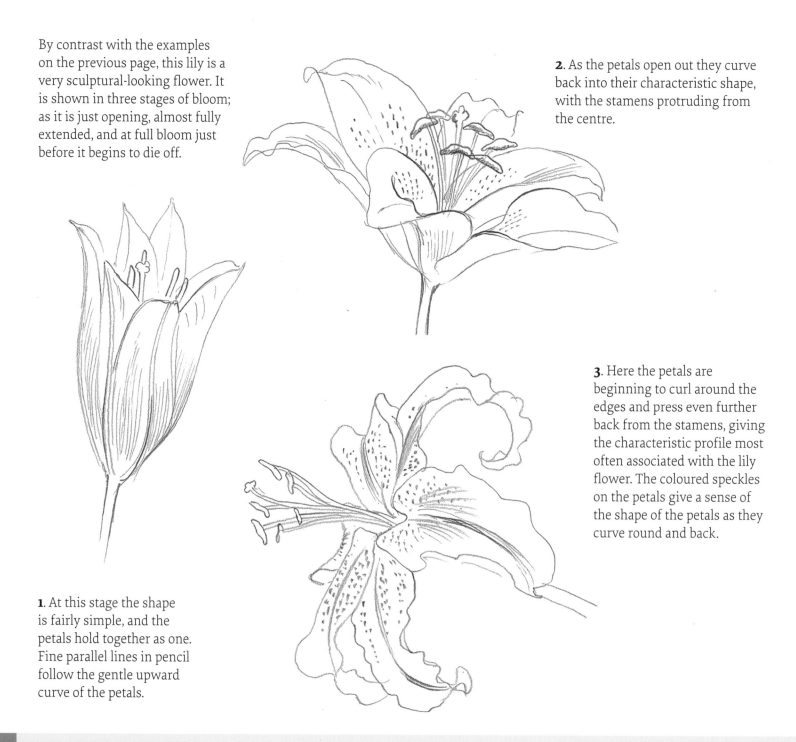

2. As the petals open out they curve back into their characteristic shape, with the stamens protruding from the centre.

3. Here the petals are beginning to curl around the edges and press even further back from the stamens, giving the characteristic profile most often associated with the lily flower. The coloured speckles on the petals give a sense of the shape of the petals as they curve round and back.

1. At this stage the shape is fairly simple, and the petals hold together as one. Fine parallel lines in pencil follow the gentle upward curve of the petals.

Potted plants are ideal subjects and give plenty of opportunity for practising the growth of the leaves and how this growth is repeated throughout the plant. As with all plants, attention to detail is important. You need to investigate how each leaf stalk connects to the main stem and how many leaves there are in each clump.

The same pattern of leaf growth can look quite different when viewed from varying angles. It is worth experimenting: drawing the plant from beneath, from above, and also side on just to give yourself experience of how the shapes alter visually.

Large plants are also ideal practice for drawing trees. They display many similar characteristics and they ease you into upping the size at which you draw.

In this example each leaf has a characteristic curl. Once you see the similarities in the pattern of the plant, the speed at which you draw will increase. It is important to feel the movement of the growth which the shape shows you through the plant and how it repeats in each stalk.

Artist's Note

Once you start drawing larger plants, you realize that drawing every leaf is very time-consuming. Some artists do just this, but most devise a way of repeating the typical leaf shape of the plant and then draw in the leaves very quickly in characteristic groups. It is not necessary to count all the leaves and render them precisely, just put in enough to make your drawing look convincing.

Trees

Even if you live in a town, you probably have some vegetation near you in a garden or a park. Go and have a look at some trees, and notice how complex they are, with their myriad leaves and branches. One student of mine, when confronted with a tree to draw, said, 'Do I have to draw every leaf?' Of course, the answer is no – but you do have to make a tree look as though it has leaves en masse.

As you can see, these first sketches help to establish the proportion and overall look of the trees without much drawing.

In the next three drawings, I've shown how you can indicate leaves with a sort of scribble technique so that they look softer and less definite than the trunk and branches (above); or you can outline whole masses of leaves and just put a tone over the areas where the shadow is deep (above right). Alternatively, you can simply outline the whole shape of the tree without worrying about the different parts (right).

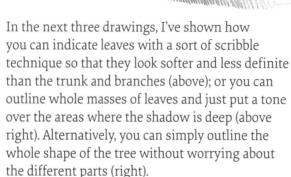

You can take the same generalizing approach when using colour, indicating large clumps of leaves according to how the light falls over the tree. In this pastel drawing the lighter green is used where the light falls on the top side of the leaves, with the darker areas underneath. The branches are visible through the masses of leaves in a few places, giving the sense of the underlying structure of the tree. We will look more at drawing trees on pages 202–3.

People

The human figure is probably the most challenging of all subjects for an artist, partly because our familiarity with it means we can see immediately when a drawing isn't convincing. Because of this, you'll need to practise drawing people much more often and with more intensity than most other subjects. However, starting isn't any more difficult, because at this stage you'll be drawing in a very simple fashion.

Hands

We begin with hands, because you can draw your own – they have the advantages of being very well-known to you and always available!

1. First, draw around your hand to familiarize yourself with its proportions on paper. Place your hand flat on the paper and carefully trace around it.

4. With the fingers bent slightly, seen from the top.

5. With the fingers spread, seen from the side.

6. And again from the other side.

3. Now, keeping your original drawing close at hand so you can check against it, place your hand flat on the drawing surface again and, next to it, make a careful copy without drawing around it. Bear in mind that your first drawing will probably be a bit too fat for reality but correct proportionately. Once you feel happy with a freehand drawing of your hand, draw it in various positions.

7. Then with the fist clenched, seen from the thumb side.

2. You won't obtain an exact rendering of your hand with this method, but you'll be able to see quite clearly from your drawing the length of the fingers contrasted with the shape of the back of the hand.

8. With the fist clenched, seen from the knuckle end.

Feet

The obvious part of the body for you to draw next is the foot because, as with your hands, you can draw your own feet quite easily – especially if you have a mirror handy to see them from various angles. There is so much less movement in the foot than in the hand that it's not such a difficult thing to draw. The greatest problem is that we don't normally look at feet much, so the shapes won't be so familiar to you.

The basic shape of the foot is a simple flattened pyramid that joins on to the leg at the top. It isn't as complex as the hand, so you won't have too much trouble getting a reasonable version of its shape.

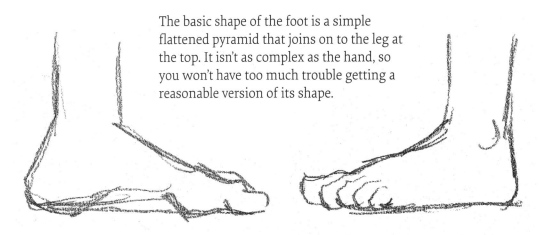

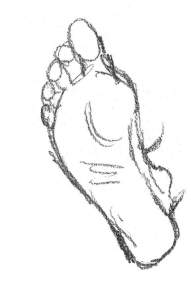

The hardest views are directly from the front or back, so you may have to look at those rather more carefully. The front isn't a problem to see if you have a mirror, but the back might be easier if it is someone else's foot.

Even the underneath of the foot can be seen in a mirror, so you shouldn't have too much difficulty.

The Head and Face

When it comes to drawing the head, a common error that novices make is to concentrate on the face without paying much attention to the rest of the skull. In fact, the rest of the head is much larger than the area occupied by the face, but people often fail to notice this because their interest is caught by the facial features.

In this drawing, the dotted line shows the limit of the area occupied by the features of the face.

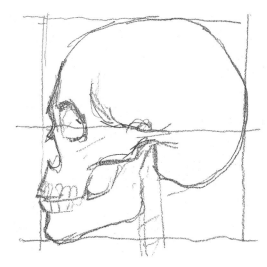

To discover the truth of this for yourself, draw a square first, then draw a skull inside it. You can copy my drawing, because you probably won't have a skull handy! Notice how the eye sockets are halfway down from the top of the skull. This is rarely spotted by novice artists. You'll find more detail on the proportions of the head on pages 154–5.

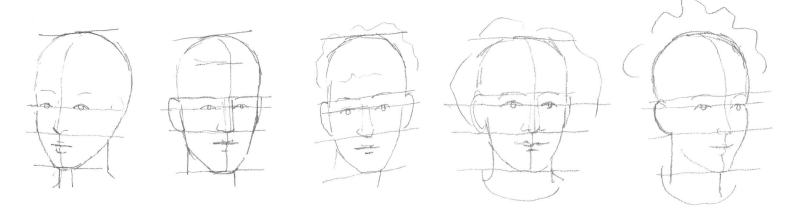

Here I have drawn the heads of five different people, which show how we all have similar head proportions and the differences only start to show with the addition of the facial features and hair.

Here I've put in all the particular features that turn these drawings into portraits of two young women and three young men. It's the finer features of the women and the hairstyles that create the differences between the main shapes of the male and female heads, but the details of the features make the heads more individual. If you met these people you wouldn't mistake one for the other, though you might not have spotted much difference in the initial drawings showing the head shapes and placement of the features.

This exercise will have helped you to realize that one face isn't more difficult than another, because all faces have a basic shape so similar that it's only the final details of the features that make them distinguishable. Always draw people as though they were the same, but bring in the individuality with sensitive delineation of the final look.

A Figure in Steps

Drawing people is not so easy as drawing plants, not least because it requires the co-operation of your friends or relatives. Most people don't like to sit still for too long, so you may have to stop drawing sooner than you would wish because your model has got tired of posing. The idea here is to attempt a whole figure including the face and clothes, so make sure your model is comfortable before you start and allow them some breaks to move around and stretch cramped muscles.

Step 1

First make a simple sketch of the position of the figure on the chair. I was sitting quite close to my subject, so the legs disappear at the lower edge of the picture. Notice how in this initial drawing the main shape of the movement through the body and the arrangement of the arms and head are already shown, albeit briefly.

Step 2

The next step is to firm up the main shapes of the figure, paying close attention to the angle of the head, the shapes of the arms and hands, and the relaxed turn of the body. By the end of this step the broad outline of the model is established.

Step 3

Now it's time to look at the details of each part of the figure, making careful note of the shapes of the head and the hair, and the way the features are arranged. Next, the way that the clothes drape around the body needs to be seen clearly, but don't put in every detail of the clothing at this stage – just the main folds that define the form underneath. Put in the hands and the parts of the chair that can be seen; in this case I could see the model's legs so I defined the main shape of these as well.

Step 4

Firm up the shapes of the body and head, so that your model starts to become recognizable. Remember that this is always a work in progress, and you don't have to end up with a highly finished piece of work. Alter or erase anything that you think is not looking like the shapes you can see, and don't worry if the drawing becomes very messy; this just means that you are beginning to observe more sharply, and the effort to correct your drawing is never wasted.

Notice that on my finished drawing the marks are very exploratory – the edge of the body is drawn with a variety of lines, not sharply defined. This allows for the fact that you can see around the edges of a three-dimensional form and so there is never really one sharp line. I have not put in much texture or shading, just enough to show the form in a simple fashion. It is still a drawing in progress, and if I could get my model to sit again in exactly the same position with the same clothes on, I could continue drawing for another period of time.

Chapter Three

FORM, TONE AND TEXTURE

This chapter is all about trying to make the objects you draw look realistic by establishing their form in more detail. In order to do this you will also have to keep working on your drawing of outline shapes.

So, starting off with carefully drawn shapes, you need to follow this up with adding tone and shading to the forms to give a feeling of solidity. This needs quite a lot of practice, so there are many variations in the objects I have given you to draw. You will also begin to see how the methods that you use in one drawing can easily be adapted for other things that at first glance seem very different. The more you can practise these methods the better you will become at drawing.

As you become more comfortable with adding tone you can begin to focus on particular types of texture and materiality, such as glass, metal, fabric, food and plants. We shall look at how to render textures using different drawing media to create different effects.

Developing Form and Tone

To start our investigations into developing form, we look at two objects, a thermos flask and a tumbler, made of metal and glass respectively. Whereas the flask needs a building up of tone to show its rounded form and the darker parts of the metal, the glass tumbler needs only minimal shading, because it is transparent.

First just draw the outline shapes of the objects and in the vacuum flask mark where the edges of the brightest and darkest areas of tone are to be. In the glass tumbler just put in the edge shapes of the moulded glass and the surface of the water.

Having done this, put in all the darkest tones on the flask as smoothly as you can. Gradually fill up all the other areas where the tones are less intense, making sure that you leave the brightest bits totally white, clean paper. If you smudge any of these white areas, use the fine edge of an eraser to clean them up. When you have covered all the areas of tone, study the whole drawing to see if you need to strengthen any of the darkest parts.

With the glass tumbler the trick is not to do too much shading. Put in the very darkest parts first, noticing that there are not very many of them. Then add the medium and lightest tones, underdoing the tone rather than overdoing it. When you think you've finished give it a careful look to see if any tones really need to be strengthened, and then stop before you overwork it.

At first you might not be very successful in your efforts but as you continue to practise you will soon develop the necessary skill to make your work look more convincing.

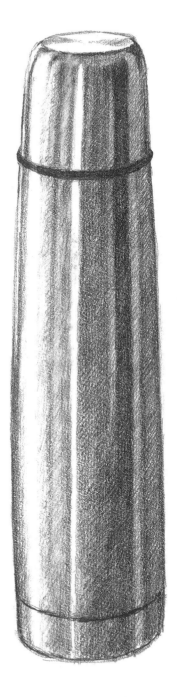

Tone on an Object

It is only once tone has been added that an object begins to look like something three-dimensional that you can handle and use. The following drawings show just how important it is to be able to use tone to describe the substance of objects.

Here I've drawn a light-coloured jug, first in outline to show how the shape alone, if well described, will give you quite a lot of information about the jug. You can see that it must be round and that it has a lip and a handle, and it appears to be on a surface, the limit of which you can see behind it.

In the next drawing all the tone has been put in to show the difference that this makes to our knowledge about the object. The space is more defined and the quality of the curve of the jug is more clearly seen so you get some feeling of its solidity.

In the next drawing I have put in all the tone on the jug but have left out the tonal background. This has the effect of making it appear to float in the space, because it hasn't any real connection with the background.

The last drawing of the jug does the opposite, making the dimensions of the object loom out of the darkness of the background, so that it's very clearly defined as light against dark. This isn't in fact realistic, but it's a good way of bringing our attention to the jug shape jumping out of the space. So you can see that tone can add or subtract quite a bit where even a simple drawing is concerned.

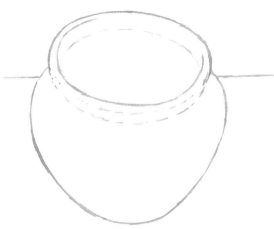

Step 1

Here I've drawn a simple brush and wash version of a white pot against a white background as an exercise in producing shade with this medium. The first step is to draw the outline of the pot with a fine-pointed brush.

Step 2

Next, put in the whole area of shadow on the pot, the surface it's resting on and the background, using one light tone only. The placement and shape of the area of highlight inside the pot is key to the success of the picture.

Step 3

Wait for the first layer of tone to dry before putting in the darker tones to emphasize the roundness of the pot, building them up with care to let the edges of the tone blend in.

Working up the Simple Object

Choose a few objects from around the house and study them in detail before drawing them slowly and carefully. The items shown here are fairly simple but with enough complexity to be a good test of your newly acquired skills.

Step 2

Put in the main areas of shade with one single tone, using a hatching technique of fine parallel lines. Pay attention to the inside of the cup and to the tones on the side of the saucer.

Step 1

First, as with the cup and saucer on page 35, draw the ellipses to show the top and bottom of the cup, and the main shape of the saucer. Draw the handle shape and the curved sides of the cup.

Step 3

Lastly, work up the tones, deepening those inside the cup and on its shadowed side, and smoothing the mid-tones with the edge of your pencil. Keep working until you get a good likeness of the shapes and reflections on the objects.

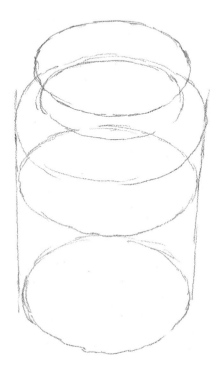

Step 2

Shade in the area that represents the tinted water. There will not be many other tones, due to the transparency of the glass.

Step 1

The next object is a glass jar containing tinted water. As before, draw the ellipses and outside edges of the jar, not forgetting to indicate the level of the water as well.

Step 3

Now indicate all the very darkest parts and also show the difference between the body of the water and the surface. Most of the darkest tones are around the lip of the jar and the indentations in the glass at the top and bottom. Finally, use an eraser to pick out any highlights you may have missed or that have been smudged.

For your next object, take something like a shoe; it will be more complex because of its structure. You could also try rendering an object in colour, like the blue-striped mug on the facing page.

Step 1

Once again, the initial task is to try to get a decent outline of the entire shape, with indications as to where the laces are and how the construction works. Keep it simple to start with.

Step 2

Now, put in sufficient details until the drawing resembles the actual shoe in front of you. The stitching is useful because it indicates the shape of the object as well.

Step 3

Next, add the tone, only this time use a more textured way of shading, to give some indication of the material; it will be a slightly coarser texture than we have used so far.

Darken the spaces between the laces, showing that there is space within the shoe.

Step 1

Once again, start this drawing of a mug by making an outline drawing. Look carefully at exactly what you see to get it as accurate as possible.

Step 2

In the second stage, if you are using a mug like this example, you will need to add the concentric circles that wrap around its diameter. Look carefully at how these lines recede from view around the sides of the mug. Once you are happy with the overall shapes and pattern, add a light colour to all the blue parts of the mug, and use a graphite pencil to indicate the shadow falling over the whole shape.

Step 3

To complete your drawing, spend plenty of time working over the areas of tone with your coloured pencils, letting the paper show through where there are bright highlights. I used the same blue pencil for all of the stripes on the mug, creating the darker tones by applying more pressure and layering the colour.

Tonal Drawing Practice

With some understanding of how form and tone can be used to create realistic-looking drawings, you can now turn your attention to some more varied objects. Consider which drawing materials are best suited to rendering the tone on these objects.

First, a drawing in ink of an apple. The build-up of tonal texture is done in a scribble technique, which seems to work well with rounded objects.

The flowers are drawn in charcoal, and the soft edges of the medium suit the quality of the plants. The slightly woolly texture of the blossoms is easily shown in this medium.

Because of its straight-edged manufacture, this toy seems a good subject for using pen and ink. You can draw most of the main tone in lines that echo the lines of the form, so lots of verticals and horizontals to start with, and then a few diagonals to deepen some areas in tone and texture.

The brush and wash technique helps with the drawing of a leather bag, its slightly squashy look being easily adapted to this technique.

A careful pencil drawing suits a white pestle and mortar, with the shadows put in as pale tones, since a light-coloured object would only have dark tones if it were subjected to very dramatic lighting.

Some trees seen over a fence are easier to draw in charcoal, because this medium is sympathetic to the soft clumps of leaves.

Here are two examples of how to put together a drawing which largely relies on tone for its effect. One is of a girl sitting in front of a fire in the evening, and the other is of a large tabby cat. Both are mostly made up of changes in tonal density rather than definite lines to show their substance; in neither of them are lines much in evidence.

Step 1

To start, draw a very simple outline of the main shapes, showing the areas of differing tones. The only point of the outlines is to make sure the proportions are correct.

Step 2

Then put in the shaded areas all as one tone, leaving white paper for the highlights. Note that the light is coming from below, which gives the girl's face an unusual look.

Step 3

Carefully darken the areas that need to be stronger until you are satisfied that the picture is strong and convincing.

Step 1

Drawing the cat is a similar exercise, except that the tone is much more descriptive of the pattern on its fur, rather than denoting a source of light. Start with an outline of its body and loosely indicate its face and stripes.

Step 3

Finally, draw into the main areas of darker tone to bring out the stripey appearance of the fur.

Step 2

Cover nearly all of the cat with a simple tone – there are very few areas of white in this picture, and they appear mainly on the face and chest.

Tonal Drawing in Colour

The following examples show some approaches to developing form and materiality with different colour media. These exercises can go on forever because you will always come across objects that you haven't drawn before, and there is always more to learn. However, try to find something made of metal, something made of glass, and something natural, like fruit or plants. With lighter or transparent objects, it can be useful to put in the immediate surroundings because they have an effect on the colour of the object itself.

This example, in pastel and chalk on toned paper, is of a glass jar on a white table-top against a darker background. The glass catches the light, so you can use a lot of white chalk here but, where there are dark tones, put them in boldly. This contrast emphasizes the transparency and materiality of the object.

Artist's Note

The trick with this type of drawing is to remember the adage 'less is more'. Don't overdo the initial stages of the drawing – simplify as much as possible and the drawing will maintain its freshness. Make sure that your deepest tones and your highlights are put in simply but boldly. You have to take chances in art, but if they don't work, don't give up trying. It is all part of the fun.

This second example, of an enamel jug in coloured pencil, is a simple shape; a cone cut off at the top with handle and spout added. The colour is white, so all you have to consider is the shadow colour and that of the background. The reason that this jug stands out so boldly is that the background colours are all stronger and darker than the jug – the feeling of it existing in three-dimensional space is due to the effect of the background colour, as much as the jug itself. The cast shadow across the table-top helps to anchor the object to the surface that it stands on. Notice how the lines of the background shapes are made softer and less distinct than the lines on the jug. This technique also helps to define the space around it.

The three examples shown here were all produced in watercolour. As we have seen it is a very flexible medium, rather difficult to start with, but easy enough to handle when you've made the first steps.

Here is an ordinary metal kettle, not very shiny, but reflective enough. First, outline the shape with the brush, using a grey colour. When that is dry, flood the main light areas at the top of the kettle in a cool light blue-grey and a warmer brown-grey for the lower parts. Don't forget to leave little areas of white paper unpainted to indicate the highlights on the handle, lid and spout. When the first colour is dry, put in a dark neutral grey on the lower part to give darker shadows, but wash it off to one side of the main body of the kettle, so that the surface appears curved. Then, sparingly, put in darker tones on the handle and lid.

The next example is of a glass; you have already attempted glasses in pencil (see pages 60–1 and 65) then in pastel (see page 72), so you know the problems involved. It is best to include the background here because glass is defined by the fact that the background colour will show through. Again, you have to leave areas of unpainted white paper around the edges of the glass and across its broader facets to mimic the reflected light that convinces the eye that this is indeed a glass object. Once you have put in the background and the brightest, lightest areas, you can put in the dark ones. This contrast between dark and light is the standard way of showing reflective surfaces. Parts of the outline can be very dark, and some left white.

When you come to fruit and vegetables, the method is similar but the contrast between dark and light is not so great. These tomatoes are painted smoothly round with the darkest tones towards the shadowed undersides. On each tomato, leave one small area of white paper almost untouched to achieve the effect of the tiny highlight that occurs on glossy objects. Add in a dark green stalk to connect the tomatoes into a bunch and a cast shadow to 'anchor' them in place.

The examples shown here use a combination of different materials: coloured chalks for the jug, and a mix of coloured pencils and coloured ink for the plant on the facing page.

The shiny texture of this glazed blue ceramic jug was best captured with white chalk highlights. I marked out the position of the highlights before shading the whole jug in blue chalk, leaving the paper blank where I wanted the brightest light. A few additional highlights in yellow chalk provided a marked contrast to the blue ceramic and added interest to the drawing.

Step 1

This vigorous plant growing at the corner of a terrace had very bright, shiny leaves. I started by outlining the main shapes of the leaves, observing whether they were pointing downwards to the earth, up to the sky or somewhere between the two. This overall direction of growth is more important than drawing every single leaf.

Step 2

I added light tone across the drawing in coloured pencil, using a brown colour for the background, dark grey for the shadowed area beneath the plant, a dark green for the centre of the plant and a yellow colour for the tips of the leaves where they caught the light. Blending the dark green and yellow gave a bright, light green also visible on the plant.

Step 3

Using a combination of coloured pencils, felt-tip pens and fineliners, I worked up the deeper tones of my drawing. For the very darkest areas in the centre of the plant, I used a dark green felt-tip and a black fineliner, and added a few dashes of orange felt-tip on the brightest leaves. I also marked out the lattice pattern of the terrace tiles very lightly with brown fineliner, giving a sense of depth to the picture.

Exercise with Paper

As you get more proficient, you will find that the marks you make when you draw any object give an effect of the material that it is made of. Here is an exercise often given to art students to test their ability to observe shape and texture, and that is to take a piece of paper, crumple it up, and then put it down and draw it as accurately as you can.

Step 1

Draw the lines or folds in the paper, paying attention to getting the sharp edges of the creases.

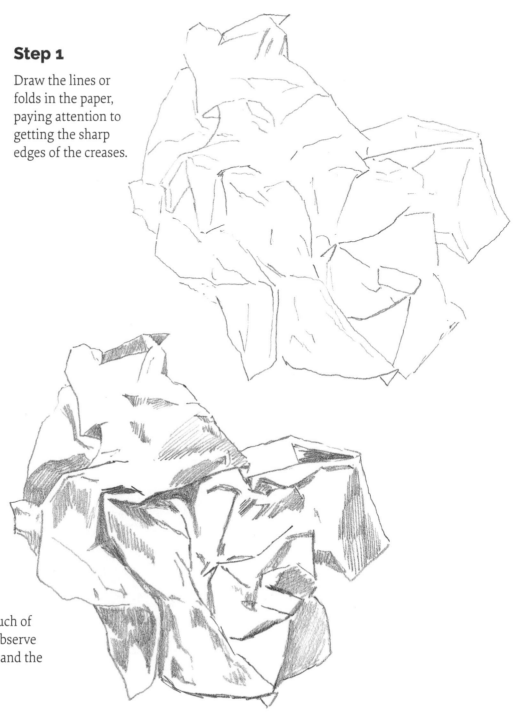

Step 2

Put in the main areas of tone. Much of the paper will remain white, so observe carefully where the shadows are and the shapes they form.

Step 3

Once you have covered each tonal area, put in any deeper shadows, capturing the contrasts between these areas. The smooth, dark surface beneath the paper helps to give the drawing a sense of depth and echoes the rest of the tonal areas.

When you have completed the last exercise, try a variation on it. Crumple a piece of paper and then open it out again. Look at it and you will see that the effect is rather like a desert landscape. Before you try to draw it, position the paper so that you have light coming from one side; this will define the facets and creases quite clearly and help you.

Follow the three steps of the previous exercise, putting in the darkest shadows last.

Practising Textures

Here we focus on developing a feel for different types of materials and transferring their textural qualities on to paper.

To start with, draw a very simple outline of the shapes of the cascading hair, getting a feeling for the way it winds and curves as it grows away from the head. It doesn't matter if you don't get some of the curves quite right as long as the main shapes are followed.

Now you can build up a texture of lines and tone to produce a convincing impression of the hair. Work in strokes following the main shapes of the curves of the hair, in some cases drawn heavier and darker and elsewhere drawn much lighter and fainter. This gradually produces the look of hair in waves. Notice how often at the edges of the mass of hair the tone looks darker, and how there is a contrast between the dark under curve and the lighter upper curve where the larger waves curl round.

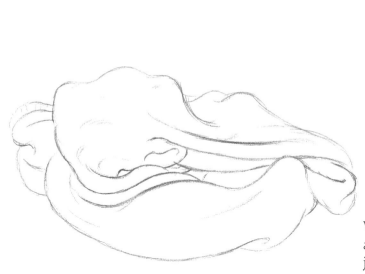

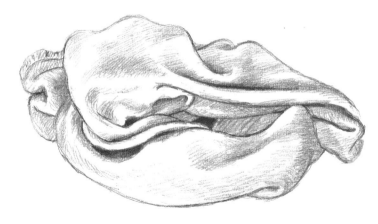

With the fabric, first notice the main folds and carefully draw them in as accurately as you can. The texture here is much simpler to draw than hair, just needing either darker or lighter tones to indicate the folds. As this particular piece of fabric is an old sweater, it can be drawn softly and slightly rough in texture to indicate the look of wool.

In the case of the basket, the difficulty is to achieve the effect of the interweaving strands without drawing every one exactly. Try to obtain a general impression with the lined-up marks so that the weaving is uniform enough without looking too clean-cut. The texture of basketwork is not very precise, and you can exploit this fact to give a good impression rather than try to draw every strand exactly. Make sure that the shaded parts are strong enough to convince the eye of the depth of the space inside and around the object. Try not to overdraw on the lighter areas so that the contrast between the two parts will work better for you.

Combining Materials

Portraying different kinds of materials in one drawing is an excellent way of honing your ability and will stand you in good stead for drawing still-life compositions. Start with some simple combinations before building up your repertoire.

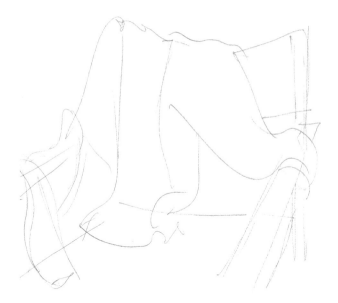

Step 1

This exercise shows mostly fabric textures, with a woollen jumper draped over a canvas chair. However the straight wooden arms of the chair provide a marked contrast to the softer textures. First draw a rough sketch to make sure you have got the mass and bulk of the subject right.

Step 2

Now make a careful outline drawing, allowing the lines to suggest the soft edges of the material as well as the shape of it. Make sure that the hard, smooth lines of the chair contrast with the texture of the sweater's outline.

Step 3

Next, make a careful all-over rendering of the main tone, not differentiating between dark and light tones at this stage.

Step 4

Lastly, build up the tonal values to give an effect of the texture and soft drape of the garment, taking care to make the chair look harder and sharper-edged than the cloth.

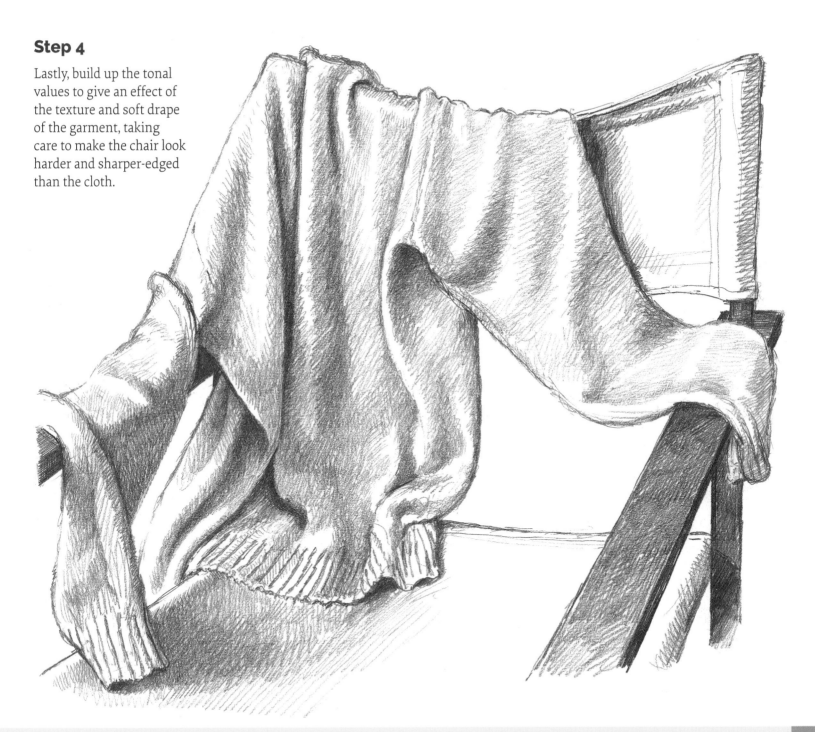

Here, notice the contrast between the hard, reflective surface of the vase and the soft and blowsy forms of the flowers. Notice how the dark background accentuates this contrast by emphasizing the pale flowers.

Step 1

Loosely sketch the main shape of the vase and flowers, using shorter, more diffuse marks for the latter.

Step 2

Next, draw everything in a more defined outline, so that you are sure that the shapes of the flowers and the vase are pretty accurate. Lightly outline the highlights and cast shadow.

Step 3

Now work over the whole picture with a light, uniform tone. Leave the lightest areas on the vase, table and flowers as white paper.

Step 4

Now work over all the areas where the shadow is deepest, so that you have all the very dark areas marked in.

Step 5

Working over the whole composition, blend in the darks and lights with mid-tones and put in any definition that is still needed. Take your time, since this is quite a complicated subject.

This drawing combines the different textures of a loaf of bread (inside and out), a small round cutting board and a bread knife, all set on a table surface. Although the colours are quite similar across the drawing, the marks used for the bread help to define its texture.

Step 1

Start by making an outline drawing of the whole arrangement, using the main colour which in this case is brown. Care should be taken over the elliptical shape of the cutting board and the angle of the knife.

Step 2

Add a light tone across the drawing, using your main colours. A gentle hatching technique should suffice for most areas, with slightly denser cross-hatching on the darker bread crust.

Step 3

Add extra layers of hatching to show the darker tones in your drawing, and indicate the areas of shadow beneath the bread and the bread knife handle using graphite pencil. The texture of the bread can be shown with small flicks of a pencil, while for the shiny surface of the bread knife use the side of your pencil lead to create finely graded shading.

Step 4

As usual, the final stage of your drawing is to work on the darker tones and highlights, blending your colours, deepening shadows and defining shapes. As a final touch, I added some dabs of white ink to show the light-coloured seeds that were scattered over the bread crust. It is worth being flexible with your materials in this way; if you stick rigidly to one medium for the whole drawing, you may miss out on the opportunity to improve your work.

Chapter Four

STILL-LIFE COMPOSITION

Once you have gained some confidence in your ability to draw various objects and convey their form and texture convincingly, the next step is to try putting together a composition of several objects and producing a still-life drawing.

One of the ways that you can arrive at an interesting still-life arrangement is to look for accidental ones around your house. I find that I often come across natural compositions of objects that have occurred by virtue of the everyday habits of living. Sometimes they are complete in themselves, while on other occasions they just need a slight alteration to make a very pleasing still life.

You'll find it useful to make separate drawings of all the objects that you choose for a still-life composition, to familiarize yourself with their shapes and textures. This sort of preparation is never wasted. The final arrangement of a still life should be made up of things that you find interesting in themselves. Don't put anything in the arrangement that you don't really want to draw. Have faith in your own taste – it really does make a difference to the intensity and quality of your work.

Last but not least, familiarize yourself with still lifes by artists that you admire to gain some wider understanding of all the possibilities and themes. The examples after master artists shown in this chapter (see pages 108–11) will set you on the right path.

Simple Still-Life Arrangements

It isn't difficult to put together a still-life arrangement, but it does require some thought and aesthetic appreciation. If you are a beginner, it's a good idea to accumulate your still-life objects gradually, with some feeling of how the final shape of the arrangement will look. So here I begin by simply choosing things that make interesting drawing problems for an artist to solve.

Next I took a bowl of oranges that was on my dresser. Fruit in a bowl is a traditional prop for still-life arrangements and presents the problem of drawing spherical objects that are pushed together by the sides of the bowl. Both of these subjects are the kind of thing that make a simple still life without any other objects being necessary; of course you might want a bit more background space to show off the quality of your drawing, but nothing else is particularly needed.

Starting with what happened to be on the top of the plan chest in my studio, I gave myself the problem of drawing a number of pencils bunched together in a glass jar. I had to find a way of showing the transparency of the pot and the variety of pencil tops poking up out of it – slightly difficult, but not so much so it would become laborious.

The next choice was more considered. I found two jugs of different shapes and sizes and placed them next to each other, turning them so that their spouts faced towards each other. The fact that one is short, curvy and dark in colour while the other is tall, straight and lighter figured in my reasons for choosing them, so here you can see how I have begun to make aesthetic judgements about even a very simple subject, whereas before I had just happened upon the still lifes.

Artist's Note

Even with the simplest of still-life subjects, you need to consider the lighting. You may run into difficulties if you start your drawing in one light and finish it in another. Consider how long your drawing might take and if it might be necessary to set up a fixed light source.

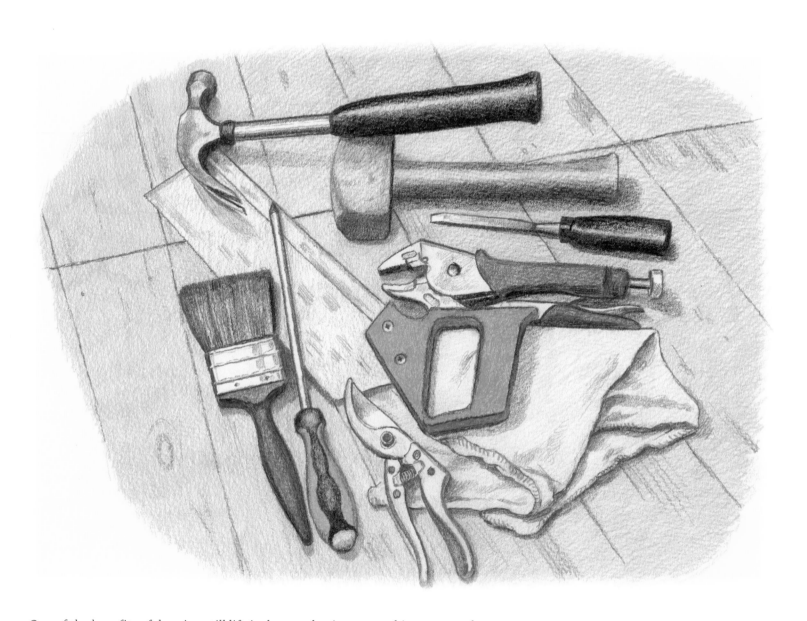

One of the benefits of drawing still life is that you begin to see subjects everywhere you look. This selection of ordinary tools might be found in any house and they are not decorative objects, but arranged close together on a surface using a little colour to enhance the composition, they make a pleasing group.

The next composition is more complicated, with numbers of cups hanging on a sideboard, glasses under the shelf and a large basketwork tray full of fruit, arranged fairly carefully. This is much more like the traditional paintings of still lifes that artists have been making for many generations.

Ephemeral Still Lifes

One of the attractions of still life is the simple, domestic views it often portrays: the tea-tray, a coat thrown over a chair. Even the most simple drawing can catch the feeling of a house or home.

Here I simply took out the contents of my pockets and put them on the table in front of me. Art students are often given a project like this, in which small objects are drawn magnified to fill out all the space. It's a good exercise that has the effect of encouraging close observation.

Here is a kitchen still-life composition in a tall format, seen against the light coming from a nearby window. It is rather quickly drawn, and looks as if it is probably a temporary arrangement.

Then we see two still-life arrangements that use the effect of clothing in the scene. On the left is a coat thrown over a basketwork chair with a pair of heavy boots on the floor nearby. They look as if they may be taken away at any moment. On the right we see an old garment like an overcoat hanging on the back of a door. Simple though it is, this arrangement gives a hint of the outdoors.

Still Life: Tea Tray

To set up a still-life arrangement, take some ordinary everyday objects that are not too complex in shape. My particular choice has been a tray with a teapot, a jug, a sugar bowl and a cup and saucer and spoon. These items have the benefit of being both immediately to hand and familiar. You can put them on a small tray to limit the area to be drawn. This means that they all overlap each other from your viewpoint, which forces a composition on the picture that you don't have to choose.

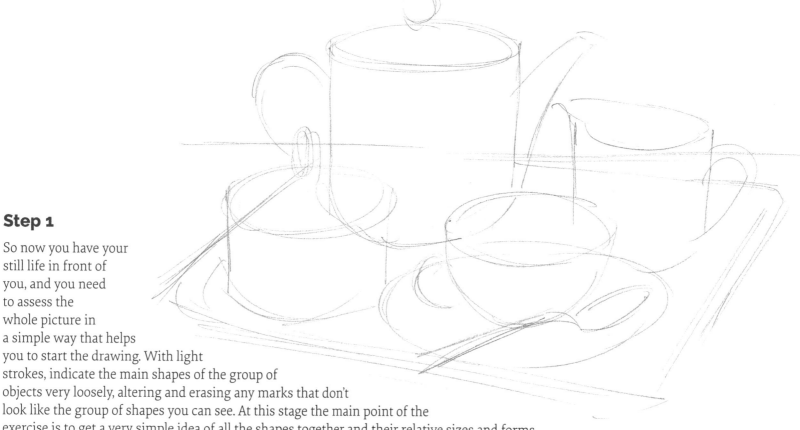

Step 1

So now you have your still life in front of you, and you need to assess the whole picture in a simple way that helps you to start the drawing. With light strokes, indicate the main shapes of the group of objects very loosely, altering and erasing any marks that don't look like the group of shapes you can see. At this stage the main point of the exercise is to get a very simple idea of all the shapes together and their relative sizes and forms.

Step 2

Having arrived at a satisfactory set of forms, you now need to define them more accurately. This means carefully drawing an outline of each object, showing how they overlap each other and how each shape is formed, this time very decisively. You will then have a complete outline picture of the whole still life. Any obvious mistakes can be carefully redrawn – it is easier to correct the mistake first and then erase the bits that are not correct.

Step 3

Now the essence of the picture is complete, you can turn to
the tonal values that will help you show the three-dimensional
qualities of the forms. At this stage, put only one depth of tone all
over, except for areas of white paper to act as highlights. When
this is finished the whole picture will take on a more solid look.

Step 4

The final stage of the drawing is an exercise in seeing which areas are much darker than all the others and which less dark. I find the best way to deal with this is to do the very darkest areas first and then gradually add any tone required to the less dark places. As you can see, quite large areas have a fairly dark tone, especially the table-top and the surface of the tray. When you are satisfied that the tones in your drawing match the tones that you can see on the objects, you know that your shading exercise has finished. If any areas are a little too dark you can gently drag an eraser across the tone to lighten it.

    This exercise may take you some time to complete, and if you find that it is becoming a chore you should stop and continue some time later – it doesn't matter if it takes longer than one session.

A Simple Arrangement in Different Media

Here we investigate how the same still-life arrangement can be drawn using different materials. I have chosen a simple set of objects: a basket, a glass bottle and a tomato, on some blue cloth. One of the cloths has a chequered pattern, but if you feel this makes it too difficult, leave it out.

When drawing in ink, less can be more, so don't overwork the subject. To begin, draw in an outline with neutral colour; I used brown, but with a grey ink for both cloth and background. Now decide what texture you will use on each of the objects to make them look convincing. Don't over-elaborate in the case of the basket. A scribble effect will help to give dimension where the shadows are. For the bottle, keep the transparent look by leaving areas of white paper showing and indicate the background through the glass shape. The tomato needs a more solid colour – use your brightest red all over, except for the highlight; I put in the front highlight with a yellowy orange, to tone it down a bit. The darker areas I put in with purple, but sparingly. The cloth can be the least drawn over, the light blue kept fairly open in texture so it doesn't dominate the picture. Lastly, the wall behind can be hatched in lightly in pale grey.

With pencil, you have to build up the colour to achieve tonal strength. Use a neutral colour for the outline then layer lighter tones over the basket, the bottle and the blue cloth. On the bottle, leave some white areas for highlights. Build up your colours from light to dark. Use your strongest, brightest red for the tomato, except for the highlights. Leave the pattern and shadows on the cloth until last.

This pastel version is drawn on a warm khaki-coloured paper, on which both strong and light colours register well. Again, sketch out the shapes. Put in the colours on the basket; keep the marks of the weave to a minimum. For the bottle, work in some dull greens, dark brown and a few touches of bright yellow for the highlights. Block in the light blue cloth and the light background wall with varying texture but enough strength to outline the shapes of the foreground objects. The tomato can be worked last as it is the most powerful colour; a strong vermilion plus crimson to give it solidity, and yellow and white spots of highlight. If some of the highlights or shadows appear too weak, strengthen them. Try not to draw over your first marks, but here and there you may need to emphasize an edge. Don't try to be too precise, and thus lose the soft-edge charm of the medium.

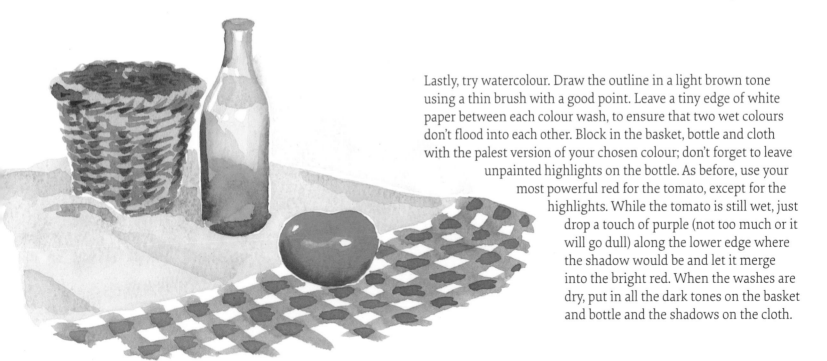

Lastly, try watercolour. Draw the outline in a light brown tone using a thin brush with a good point. Leave a tiny edge of white paper between each colour wash, to ensure that two wet colours don't flood into each other. Block in the basket, bottle and cloth with the palest version of your chosen colour; don't forget to leave unpainted highlights on the bottle. As before, use your most powerful red for the tomato, except for the highlights. While the tomato is still wet, just drop a touch of purple (not too much or it will go dull) along the lower edge where the shadow would be and let it merge into the bright red. When the washes are dry, put in all the dark tones on the basket and bottle and the shadows on the cloth.

A Still Life in Coloured Pencil

When you assemble a still life you have first of all to decide on what effect you want your picture to have. For this example, an unusual viewpoint and a muted colour palette make for a striking composition.

Step 1

I collected together a number of pots that I felt would make an interesting arrangement against the backlight of a window. I chose large metal and pottery objects, which were all fairly light in colour. As they were all circular in shape, I decided that I would play on this feature by choosing the perspective of looking down on them when they were close to me, so that the deeper shadows in the interiors of the pots gave a sort of repeat motif and were very dominant in the picture.

   As all the items were lit from behind, the main light was diffused and helped to even out the colour values. I decided that I didn't want many strong colours, aiming instead for a rather muted piece of work.

This pot has vertical sides and is a simple shape. Because it is light in colour, the interior will not look too dark.

The conical pot with the green interior is the only splash of bright colour in the composition but, as it is mainly in shadow, it is not too dominant.

The large white enamelled jug is a good sturdy shape and will have a darker interior due to the half guard around the top. The enamel is slightly chipped.

The light-coloured wooden bowl, which is smooth and chunky, will give a touch of subdued colour.

The drinking tankard, which is made from pewter, is the darkest object in the composition. Its interior looks almost black in contrast to the other objects.

Step 2

Placing these objects close together, well below my eye-level, I got a repeated pattern of circular, cylindrical shapes, with the light behind them bouncing off the light surface they are standing on. Notice the arrows showing the direction of the light which means that all the shadows are facing the viewer. Draw a sketchy outline of your own arrangement before starting on your finished drawing.

Step 3

The light colour of each of these objects, and the light background, are assets when using coloured pencil. Because with pencil you can be quite precise in your outline, take your time to get the shapes exactly right in relation to each other. Remember that the space between the objects is as important as the shapes of the objects themselves. Don't get too heavy with your shading or tone – in my arrangement only the tankard and the jug call for strong, dark colours. Notice that the darkest part of this pale still life is the interiors of the pots.

A Still Life in Pen and Ink

In this exercise you are going to take on the challenge of drawing a complete composition in pen and ink. Don't attempt a large-scale drawing at first – when you are more practised in the medium you can expand the size of your drawings, but it will take time.

I took a fairly simple still-life composition which does however have quite dark tones in it. This means that I had to work quite fast to get all the areas of tone built up to my satisfaction. If you want to avoid a lot of mark-making, choose a more brightly lit subject.

One of the tricky things about ink is its finality, which means that before you start on the ink drawing you may want to draw the outline in pencil to ensure that you have got the shapes right. This is how most commercial drawing in ink is done. You can then rub out the pencil before you proceed with the rest of the drawing. Drawing in ink without first drawing in pencil is fun, but is something you can try out when the result is less critical.

Step 1

Having produced a pencil outline of your composition, go over it very lightly in ink as shown here.

Step 2

Then build a simple light tone over all the parts that are not highlighted, using vertical lines. As you can see the outline almost disappears when you do this, so don't make your lines too heavy or you will find it hard to see your composition amid the tone.

Step 3

Now comes the build-up, using a dense cross-hatching technique. Put in the slightly darker tone with multiple diagonal lines and then the next darkest with horizontal lines and so on, with lines going in the opposite diagonal to build even denser shadows. When you have done lines vertically, horizontally and in both diagonals, you will have to use strokes going in as many directions as you can to build up the very darkest shadows. Use curved lines as well and scribbly marks to fill up any areas that look too light in tone. This will all take quite some time, so you have to be prepared to put aside time for this medium.

Themed Still Lifes

Choosing a still-life theme can help to focus the mind of the artist, because it limits the type of object that can be used. Also the viewer can find satisfaction in being able to recognize the connection between the objects. In a way a themed still life is like a narrative; it tells a story about a particular subject, which adds a point of interest that otherwise would not be there.

Vanitas

Vanitas pictures remind the viewer that happiness, earthly possessions and indeed life itself are transient; death is inevitable. The objects within them have symbolic meanings and there is often religious iconography. The genre reached its zenith in the Netherlands in the 16th and 17th centuries, but *vanitas* paintings were common in medieval times and artists today still produce them, even in our more secular age when our lives are longer than people could expect in earlier centuries.

This *vanitas* picture, after 17th-century Dutch painter Pieter Claesz (1597–1660), is dominated by the human skull, a common feature in this style of painting, and a toppled glass symbolizing the fragility and brevity of life.

Food

Of all the objects most people have around them in their homes, some of the most obviously suitable in terms of contrast of shape and texture are everyday things connected with eating, including food, utensils, crockery and cutlery. The traditional pictures of this subject often show food ready for the preparation of a meal.

Here is a still life that puts simple vegetables centre-stage, but as you can see the 17th-century Flemish painter Frans Snyders (1579–1657) has done his subject justice, producing a rich, crowded composition.

The Sea

Still lifes can be used to summon the atmosphere of a place, despite not showing any elements of landscape.

In the still life of seashells on a shelf by Adrian Coorte (1685–1723), the sea is nowhere to be seen. The elegant beauty of these sea creatures' exo-skeletons makes an attractive picture in its own right, apart from the pleasing connotations of the ocean.

The Arts and Music

Artists are naturally drawn to the themes of art and music for a still life. In earlier times, when music could only be heard in the home by virtue of someone playing an instrument, most cultured households would have had several members able to provide musical entertainment. Consequently, there was no shortage of instruments to form a still life – and for objects connected with the theme of art, all painters had to do was look around them.

Jean-Baptiste-Siméon Chardin (1699–1779) was a very famous still-life painter in 18th-century France, and in the picture on the right he is taking as his theme the attributes of the arts. The whole group is presided over by a statuette of Mercury or Hermes. This type of symbolic theme was very popular at the time.

Music was a very popular subject for a still life in the 17th and 18th centuries, possibly because there were so many new varieties of instruments being designed and made. This is an example after the French artist Pierre Huillot (1674–1751).

This composition after an unknown 18th-century artist shows shelves of music books and sheet music strewn over them. Again there is a musical theme, but this time the picture has a more scholarly look because this is where the composer is working to produce the raw material that instruments will eventually play.

Draw a Themed Still Life

As you might expect, I chose for my themed still life a set of artists' materials, so here I have put together a palette, some brushes and palette knives, some paints, a couple of canvases and bottles of painting mediums. At the last moment, I added a pomegranate just to give a different shape to the scene.

Step 1

My first drawing is a very rough outline of the composition to see if it would work as a picture. I stood a canvas and a small picture frame against the back wall, then placed a palette bang in the middle of the background to help set the scene. In front of this I placed a jar full of paintbrushes to make a more vertical statement. Next to it is a jar of pencils and a couple of bottles of varnish and turpentine. Scattered across the foreground is a small canvas with a smaller frame under it, plus a few large brushes, a couple of palette knives and some tubes of oil paint. Just to the left of the whole arrangement is the pomegranate, but it could have been anything with a rounded shape, which I felt might be useful. So now I have got some idea of how the final composition will look.

Step 2

My next task was to draw up the whole arrangement in line, making sure that everything was in proportion and the right shape. It's at this stage that you can erase any parts that don't look right and correct them, and I can't emphasize too much how important it is to continue correcting until you are satisfied with the results. This is the way that you improve your drawing systematically.

Step 3

The next stage was to put in tone over all the areas that seemed to be in shadow of some sort without worrying at this stage how dark or light it was. This was simply to mark out the areas that read as tone.

Step 4

Finally I deepened and varied all the tonal areas to suit what I could see. Some edges were much stronger than others, so I adapted their intensity by softening with an eraser or strengthening with darker marks.

A Themed Still Life in Mixed Media

This still life of toys uses drawing materials that are appropriate to the subject matter. Felt-tip pens give a strong, saturated tone and are often used by children, so these are employed to provide the brightest colours, along with pencil, fineliner pens and a little chalk to add depth.

Step 1

Begin by setting up your still life using a range of toys, deliberately creating a messy look so as to leave the impression that a child had just finished playing with them. In my example, the doll and the bear are the main centres of interest and appear to be looking at each other across the picture. This makes for an interesting dynamic and gives the image a liveliness that would be missing if these two characters were lying on the floor. Once you are happy with the composition, make a very careful outline drawing. I made mine using a brown fineliner pen, but you may feel more comfortable starting off in pencil before committing to an ink line.

Step 2

In the second stage, add flat planes of colour using felt-tip pens. They give strong coverage and bright colours and will quickly transform your image. Don't be afraid to choose colours that are even brighter than the original toys, as the colours will add to the overall effect of playfulness.

Step 3

The image may be looking rather flat at this stage, so it is time to add some depth. Work over each object, adding the areas of light and shade to give it form. I used various materials to do this; chalk highlights, small areas of hatching and cross-hatching in pencil and fineliner pen, and dabs and dashes of felt-tip pen. Finally add a background colour to bring the composition together. I chose a simple grey surface with no features, so as not to detract from the colourful toys.

Chapter Five

DRAWING IN YOUR HOME AND LOCAL AREA

Making the interior of your home your subject is the logical progression from the still-life work that you've done so far. You'll find that sometimes your drawings may appear rather awkward until you've discovered how best to tackle a view of a room and its furniture, but don't let that put you off – all artists have to go through the process of deciding exactly how much to show in a drawing. Notice how the examples after master artists show what at first glance seem to be quite ordinary scenes but manage by their acute perception to make the interior look potent and full of interest.

To start the chapter we shall look at how to construct the perspective view necessary to bring depth and space into your drawings. An understanding of perspective is essential as you begin to tackle larger scenes.

Also in this chapter we shall start to look at subjects outside the house. To make the transition easy, my advice is to step out into the garden or into your own street and try to draw what you see every day. To start with I suggest taking just one or two obvious bits and pieces of a scene, rather than try to complete a whole picture at once; little details or a piece of street furniture such as a pillarbox can be quite fascinating to draw once you start to study them.

When you feel confident enough to produce a simple scene, go for something that's familiar and local. Drawing outside will take a little more planning than you have so far required but, if you stay close to home, carrying your drawing equipment and a portable stool will be easier and you can easily retire if the weather turns against you.

One-Point Perspective

One-point perspective is the simplest form of perspective and often the only one you need to know when you're drawing subjects from close quarters.

To start a one-point perspective drawing, for example of a room, you first need to establish a horizon line, or eye level. Perpendicular to that, near the middle of the horizon, a vertical line represents your viewing point. Then, to construct the room, you need a rectangle with the two lines crossing near the centre of it – don't place them exactly in the middle, or it will look a bit too contrived. Now draw lines from the centre point where the horizon and vertical meet to pass through the corners of your rectangle.

From this point you can now construct lines as shown, to place the position of a door on one side wall and two windows on the opposite wall.

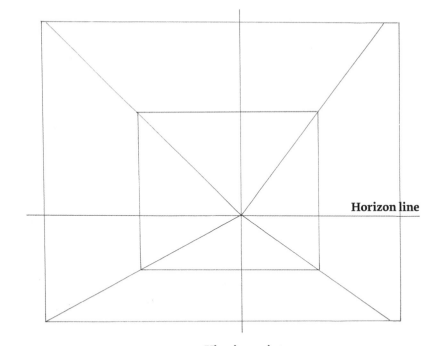

Horizon line

Viewing point

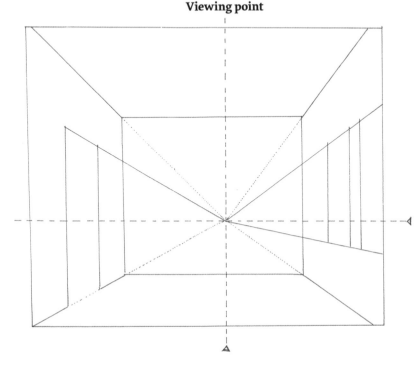

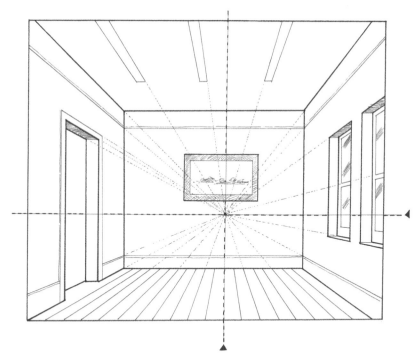

If you imagine yourself in an empty room, standing not quite in the middle, you might see something like this diagram, based on the perspective lines you've just established. Here there's a low eye level, which must mean that you're sitting down, and the room has a door to your left and two windows to your right. It has bare floorboards and strip lighting on the ceiling. There's a large picture frame hanging on the far wall.

Notice how the vertical line indicates your viewing position and the horizontal one your eye level. All the floorboards seem to slope towards the centre point, known as the vanishing point. The lines of the skirting boards and the cornice rail on the walls to each side all slope towards this centre point also, as do the tops and bottoms of the door and the windows. In other words, except for the lines which are vertical or horizontal, all lines slope towards the centre point – which is why it is called one-point perspective.

This diagram gives a good idea of how you can set about constructing a room that appears to have depth and space. Now go and stand or sit in a room of your home and see if you can envisage where imaginary horizontal and vertical lines representing your eye level and viewing position cross; this is the vanishing point for the perspective, to which all the lines that aren't vertical or horizontal will slope. Even the furniture is included in this as long as it's square on to the outlines of the room.

Here's a vast interior of an old medieval church that shows how one-point perspective works, even with an unusual building such as this. I've purposely left out any furniture in the drawing so that you can see where the perspective lines of the roof, windows and columns all join at one point, showing our eye level and viewing point.

Two-Point Perspective

When you draw outdoors you need an extra measure of perspective, because you're dealing with much bigger spaces and with large objects such as buildings and cars. This means that you need to use two-point perspective, which will enable you to construct buildings that look convincing.

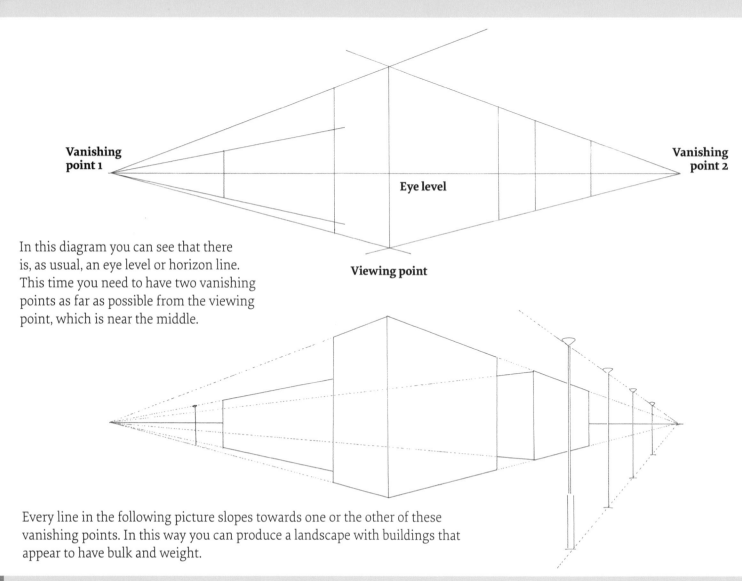

Vanishing point 1

Vanishing point 2

Eye level

Viewing point

In this diagram you can see that there is, as usual, an eye level or horizon line. This time you need to have two vanishing points as far as possible from the viewing point, which is near the middle.

Every line in the following picture slopes towards one or the other of these vanishing points. In this way you can produce a landscape with buildings that appear to have bulk and weight.

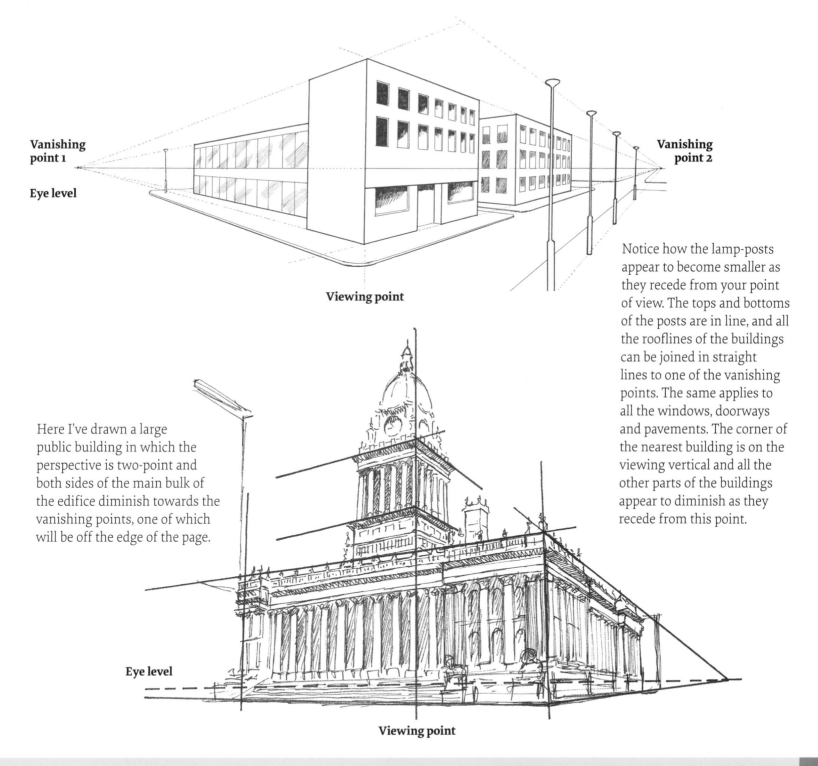

Vanishing point 1

Eye level

Vanishing point 2

Viewing point

Notice how the lamp-posts appear to become smaller as they recede from your point of view. The tops and bottoms of the posts are in line, and all the rooflines of the buildings can be joined in straight lines to one of the vanishing points. The same applies to all the windows, doorways and pavements. The corner of the nearest building is on the viewing vertical and all the other parts of the buildings appear to diminish as they recede from this point.

Here I've drawn a large public building in which the perspective is two-point and both sides of the main bulk of the edifice diminish towards the vanishing points, one of which will be off the edge of the page.

Eye level

Viewing point

Three-Point Perspective

While one-point and two-point perspective are generally all you'll need, if you want to draw very tall buildings you may have to bring in a third point of perspective.

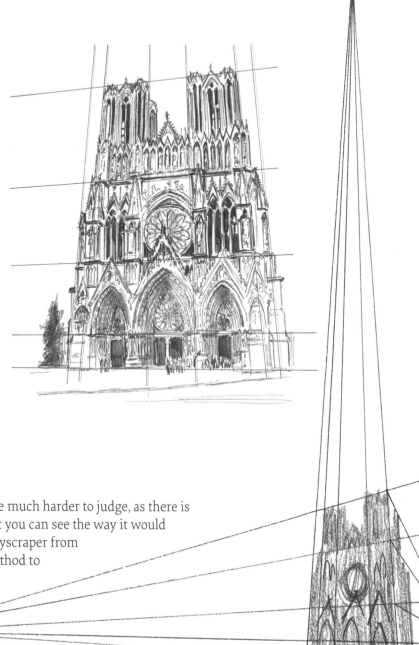

This enormous cathedral at Reims in France is a case for three-point perspective. Because of the great height of the building and the fact that the viewpoint is so close, a third vanishing point is needed high up in the sky above the cathedral. All the vertically sloping lines along the sides of the building must eventually meet at a point somewhere above it that's off the paper.

A very high vanishing point is of course much harder to judge, as there is nothing on which to fix your point. But you can see the way it would work, and if you ever have to draw a skyscraper from close to, you would have to use this method to make sense of it.

Aerial Perspective

Another rule of perspective is that as an object recedes from the viewer, it becomes less defined and less intense, thus both softer outlines and lighter texture and tone are required when we draw an object that is a long way off. These techniques help to cheat the eye and convince the viewer they are looking into a depth when they are in fact gazing at a flat surface.

Look at the drawing below and note how the use of aerial perspective and a few simple techniques gives the eye an impression of space moving out into the distance.

The tree in the middle ground has less texture and intensity than the bush.

The trees in the further distance are less well defined and more generalized in shape.

The hills in the background are softer and fainter in definition.

The nearest bush is still fairly strong in texture, in contrast to the tree.

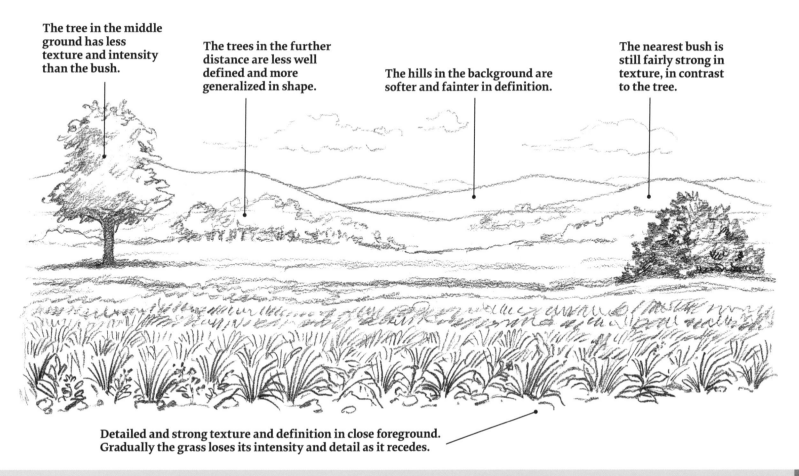

Detailed and strong texture and definition in close foreground. Gradually the grass loses its intensity and detail as it recedes.

Drawing Around the House

I started this exploration of interiors by walking around my own house and drawing small areas of the rooms from different angles and from both a standing and sitting position to give me different eye levels. Some views are quite restricted and others more expansive, but they demonstrate that even in your own house you'll find many possible subjects for a drawing. Don't worry too much if the results are rather uninteresting as pictures – the point is to practise drawing some larger objects and spaces, and also to introduce some perspective.

My first view was of an open sitting area at the back of our house. The perspective is shown mostly in the lines of the floorboards and in shapes of the dresser and window. The cupboards and chairs give scope to achieve a three-dimensional effect to add to that given by the perspective.

The next area I chose was tricky because it was halfway up the stairs and the perspective view was slightly unusual. One way to check out your own basic drawing is to take a photograph to refer back to. The top end of the stairs was well lit, while the bottom stairs in the hall were much darker in comparison. This helps to give some feeling of depth to the composition, with the banister rail sharply defined against the gloom.

Another room in my own house – a bedroom this time, which is mainly interesting for the view through to another door and the row of paintings on the wall, which help to define the space.

Next, moving in close to some objects in a room, I chose to draw the remains of breakfast on a large table, with a bowl of fruit and the tops of chairs around the edge of the table. The interesting thing about this is that it suggests a narrative of the ongoing life of the people inhabiting the house. These accidental still-life pictures are often more potent than an arranged one.

For the next view, I have done a perspective construction to give you some idea as to how the dynamics of the picture will work. This can be done with any interior, although some have more obvious perspective than others. This one, which gives us a view down the length of a table, does demand that perspective is taken into account.

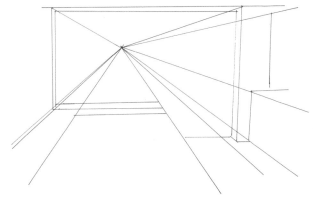

In the finished drawing below you can see how the perspective works, with the table cleared and the floorboards receding towards the windows. The light coming in from the windows and bouncing off the tabletop contrasts with the darker, shadowed areas of the walls.

Here is another perspective diagram to show how the construction of the scene gives more depth to the picture of my kitchen on the right – another area which is often the site of an interesting accidental still life.

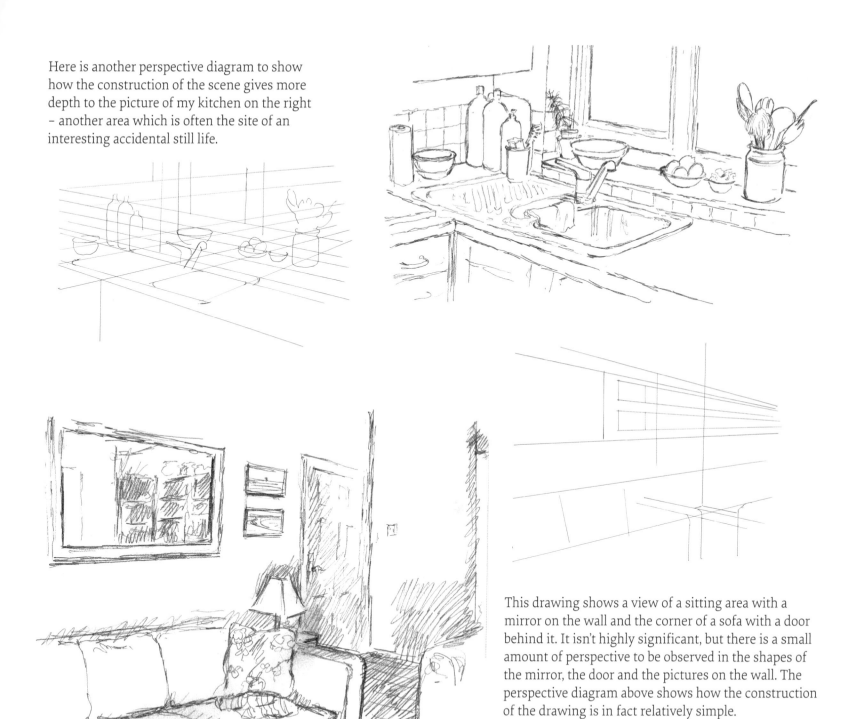

This drawing shows a view of a sitting area with a mirror on the wall and the corner of a sofa with a door behind it. It isn't highly significant, but there is a small amount of perspective to be observed in the shapes of the mirror, the door and the pictures on the wall. The perspective diagram above shows how the construction of the drawing is in fact relatively simple.

An Interior in Steps

Step 1

The first step is a perspective drawing of the structure of the room from where I am seeing it. As so many of the parts of the room are rectangular in shape, it's not too difficult to produce a perspective. This is a very ordinary room, with no pretensions to grandeur or eccentricity.

Step 2

Having got the feel of the perspective, I can now go ahead and start to
draw in all the main shapes of the furniture, walls, ceiling and floor,
keeping the outline as simple as possible without missing anything.

Step 3

Having arrived at a point where I am satisfied with the accuracy of the drawing – not without a few erasures of misjudged marks – I can now go ahead with the next stage, which is to put in all the areas of shadow in one light tone, which starts to give body to the scene.

Step 4

Finally I have to build up the real tonal values, which are sometimes strong and dark and sometimes light and gentle. When you feel that the solidity of the scene has been achieved in your own drawing, stand back to see whether your picture holds together visually. You may have to soften or strengthen some edges, or build up the very darkest tones more intensely.

An Interior in Colour

Here is an example of how you might approach an interior scene using colour, in this case coloured pens. A kitchen is very much the workaday room in the house, but that is no reason to overlook it as a subject for your drawings. In this scene you can leave all the paraphernalia of kitchen appliances and washing up material in place as you are not aiming for a slick or finished look. Instead, use bright colours and a lively cross-hatching style across all of the surfaces.

Step 1

Whether you are drawing your own kitchen or following my example, start with a careful outline drawing, taking care to get the angles of the receding worktops and cupboards correct.

Step 2

Make a selection of bright fineliner pens and use a hatching technique to cover the various surfaces of the kitchen. You can exaggerate the colours or invent them, especially if your own kitchen is monochrome. In my scene the window area offered another chance to add colour, and I used a bright yellow felt-tip to suggest the glare of the morning sun streaming through into the kitchen.

Step 3

Now work over your drawing, adding the mid-tones. Identify the areas of shadow and cover them with a relatively even tone, using a hatching technique. Some of the darkest areas, such as the cavity of the sink and beneath the wall cupboards, may require extra hatching. At this stage your scene should start to have a sense of depth.

Step 4

The final stage is to go over the whole drawing again, adding the darkest tones with cross-hatching and adding an extra colour to some areas to give your composition a lift.

Interiors after Master Artists

The examples I have chosen are mainly after 19th- and 20th-century artists. Many of us live in houses of a similar shape and construction today, or indeed we live in houses built during those centuries.

The thing to notice about these pictures is that the artists have taken trouble not to produce a banal picture, but to look at the spaces available and capitalize on them. On these pages, for example, the 19th-century Danish artist Vilhelm Hammershøi (1864–1916) has the doors open in one picture so that we can see right through the house, but in the other he shows a large blank wall with all the furniture down in the lower right-hand quarter of the composition.

In this picture after Hammershøi, the very blank wall is defined by some wood panelling, with a cluster of furniture in the lower part of the scene. A good side-light coming from an out-of-sight window helps show the dimensions of the space.

In this scene Hammershøi takes a view through some doors to a distant window. The interest here is very much in the space described by the various areas of dark and light in the rooms shown. Apart from the chair on the left, no furniture is shown.

Here is a view after French artist Edouard Vuillard (1868–1940) of a room with a fireplace, a side table and a good deal of clutter, including pictures on the walls and various objects piled on the table and mantelpiece.

Here, Vuillard's view of an attic room shows the spread of furniture across the far end of the space. The interior roof space provides a nice perspective challenge, as does the tabletop in the foreground.

This famous interior after Vincent Van Gogh (1853-90) is called *The Bedroom*, showing a simple room that the artist decorated himself in his house in Arles in the south of France. Van Gogh has deliberately omitted shadows from underneath the furniture, which has the effect of flattening the image and making it look slightly unrealistic. His emphasis is instead on the colours and feel of the space.

Stepping Out

Your first landscape can be the view out of your window or a rendering of your own garden. Consider these three very close viewpoints which take advantage of your view being restricted by the window frame, or the limits of your garden fence. So don't try to run before you can walk – try out the easiest view that you can find. It is a good test of your ability to make an adequate picture from a limited viewpoint.

This is a slightly simplified, redrawn version of a view from a window by Pierre Bonnard (1867–1947), which I've rendered in watercolour. The view is of darkening skies filled with rain clouds, with red-roofed, white-stuccoed houses in the middle ground. Beyond these are indistinct tree-covered hills. On the table in the foreground, there is a pile of books, an ink bottle and a pen and paper. The interest is in the transition from interior to exterior, suggesting space beyond the cluttered foreground.

A more difficult version of this theme is taken from *Train Landscape* by Eric Ravilious (1903–42), here recreated in coloured inks. Beyond the homely interior of an old railway carriage is glimpsed the panorama of a Wiltshire landscape with its famed white horse cut out of the chalk downs. Any train journey allows you to draw a changing landscape. You have to be quick to get enough down so that when you get home you have an accurate reminder to work up into a finished drawing.

This view – drawn in coloured pencils – is from a position on the raised decking immediately outside my own back door. We can see a bit of the Mediterranean pine and fig tree in one corner, my studio/summerhouse and the potting shed. I put the garden chairs on the lawn just to give the scene a point of focus. Your garden or backyard doesn't have to be particularly interesting or shown when the weather is good to make a worthwhile drawing or painting.

Sketching in Your Local Area

At some stage in your artistic endeavours you're going to want to move right outside and draw from a wider scene. The best way to make it a natural progression is to start at the easiest place and go into your garden or near neighbourhood, not to rush off and find a place of great scenic beauty – that can come at a later stage. If you have no experience of drawing out of doors, a wonderful panorama can be a bit daunting and trying one too soon will dent your confidence.

Not far from my house I drew some rooftops, a railway bridge and a group of cars parked along the road. Keeping the drawing simple, I immediately began to get a feel for the space and its general ambience – not at all neat and tidy, but rather haphazard.

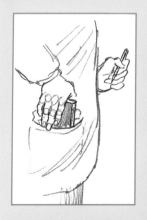

On another outing I concentrated on some street furniture, such as this letterbox, and then drew some roadside trees.

These drawings of a corrugated iron hut by the seashore and a railway bridge have a quality of emptiness, as though something were waiting to happen – for someone to enter or leave the hut, for example, or for a train to run under the bridge.

Gathering Ideas

As you gain confidence, you can try sketching various scenes to test which you might develop into a more finished drawing. Choosing a scene close to home means you can easily retire if the weather turns against you. Also, because of its proximity, you can easily go back and look again if your first efforts don't satisfy.

This cycle-path and pedestrian walk are near my home – you don't have to go far from your house to find an interesting scene that can be made into a good landscape piece. It may not have great spatial qualities, but smaller spaces can make very interesting compositions.

While roaming around central London, I came across these old Dickensian buildings near London Bridge that made a nice change from all the more recent architecture.

Back in the suburbs, this was the entrance to a primary school, which was tucked away behind the corner.

Here is the entrance to a large recreation ground, usually full of footballers, dog-walkers or cricketers. The shaded path opening out into the playing fields makes a pleasing composition.

Artist's Note

In the instance of a familiar landscape, you need to remember one of the key points about drawing: make sure you choose an area that holds some interest for you, or else you risk becoming bored with your efforts. As this always leads to a less interesting work, take a little time to choose your scene and you will be rewarded with more attractive pictures.

There is a common near Guildford, in Surrey, where my sister lives. This is an ink-drawn version of one of the painted sketches I did during a morning expedition there with her. It is essentially a very simple view, looking across the common to houses on the other side, with a row of large trees to the left and a park bench immediately in front of me. When you can show things simply but drawn well, you have gone further into the learning process towards tackling more complex situations.

A Local Scene

This scene near my house shows the typical suburban landscape of housing, roads, trees and gardens that is the type of area many of us inhabit. Of course, if you live out in the country or by the seaside, you can take advantage of your situation to bring in the greater glories of nature.

Step 1

First, as always, I made a quick sketch to get the area that I was going to draw clear in my own mind. There was a patch of grass right in front of me with a road curving away and plenty of trees around.

Step 2

Then with more care, attempting to get the perspective accurate, I drew a careful outline of all the parts of the scene, so I could differentiate between trees, bushes, pavement, grass and houses.

Step 3

I put in the main tone all over the picture, not yet differentiating between the darkest and lighter tones. This gave me a good idea as to where the greatest emphasis in the spatial qualities of the scene could be made.

Step 4

Next I built up the darkest areas with more and more tone. These were mostly parts of the houses and the evergreen trees. I was lucky to have a very dark yew tree on the right-hand side of the picture which acted as a framing device and I emphasized the overhanging leaves at the top of the picture a bit more to also help frame the scene. This is the sort of artistic licence that can greatly help a drawing.

Chapter Six

DRAWING PEOPLE

Catching someone's physical likeness is a particular skill, and managing to convey something of the sitter's character as well marks out a great portrait from a merely good one. No one will know whether you have produced a still-life set-up accurately, but your portrait subjects and their acquaintances will certainly have a view as to your degree of success.

Don't be deterred if at first your drawings don't look very much like your subjects, since this field of drawing is one of the more difficult. Keep at it, and with practice and hard work you should eventually be able to produce good likenesses of your sitters. This chapter starts you off with the basic proportions of the head, before looking at the facial features in detail and how you can plan out a portrait drawing.

We shall then move on to the proportions of the human figure so that you can try your hand at full-figure studies. Don't reject the use of photography to help here, although your own perception in studies drawn from life will ultimately give you more information than even the finest photographs.

The hardest thing to show accurately is movement, and there are no short cuts to observing what happens when a body is in motion. This observation is not only crucial to the artistic process but also endlessly fascinating.

The Head: Proportions

Most of the significant differences evident in the face are due to variations in the fleshy parts rather than in the underlying bone structure. However, the forehead, cheekbones and teeth can be more prominent in some people than in others. A child shows a smaller jaw, which is the last part of the bone structure of the head to develop.

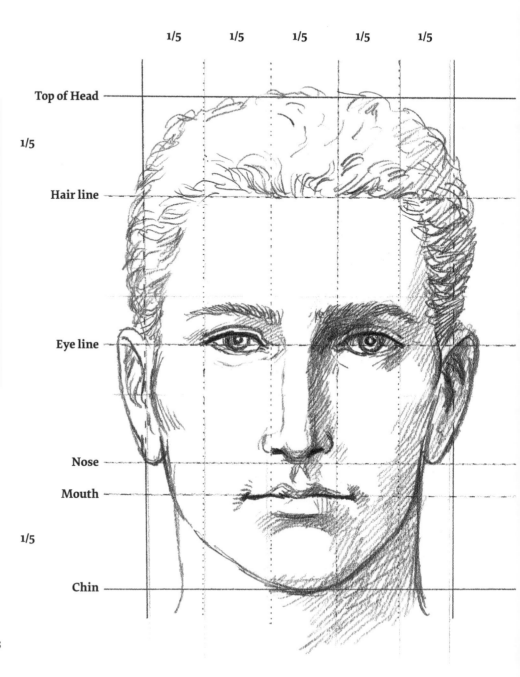

The main divisions proportionally can be clearly seen here. The eyes are half-way down the head and the length of the nose is about a quarter of the full length of the head. The mouth is about one fifth of the length of the head from the base of the chin if we measure to where the lips part. The width of the head when looked at full on and in profile is about three-quarters of the length of the head.

When a subject is viewed face on, the distance between the eyes is one-fifth of the width of the head. The length of each eye from corner to corner is also one-fifth of the width of the head.

Unless there is balding, the hair takes up about half the area of the head. This is calculated diagonally from the top of the forehead to the back of the neck, as shown.

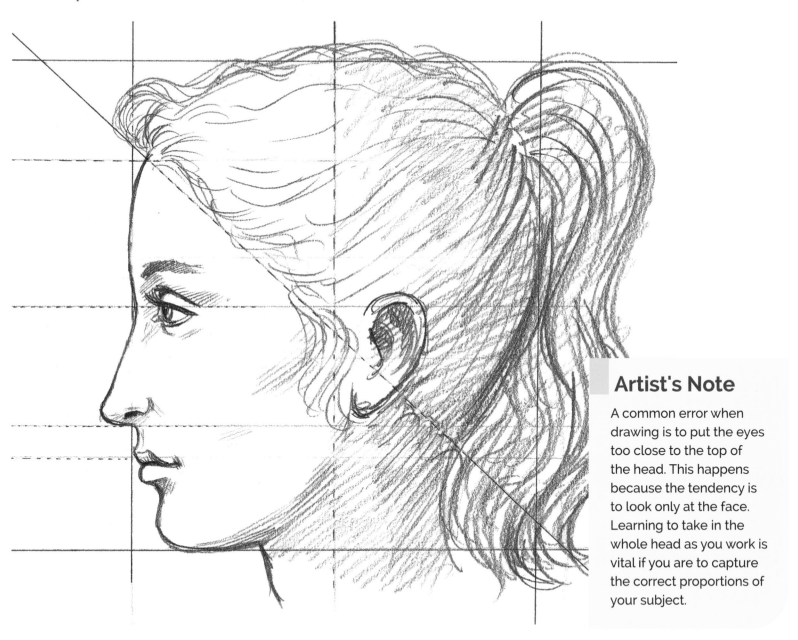

Artist's Note

A common error when drawing is to put the eyes too close to the top of the head. This happens because the tendency is to look only at the face. Learning to take in the whole head as you work is vital if you are to capture the correct proportions of your subject.

The Head from All Angles

Now for a few examples of heads in different positions which you will need to study, because you won't necessarily find your subjects' heads in exactly the full-face or profile version. Some of these are seen from slightly below and some from slightly above. The former show the projection of the jaw and the nose seems to be shorter and almost blocking out some of the eye; the latter show more of the top of the head and the mouth tends to disappear under the projection of the nose.

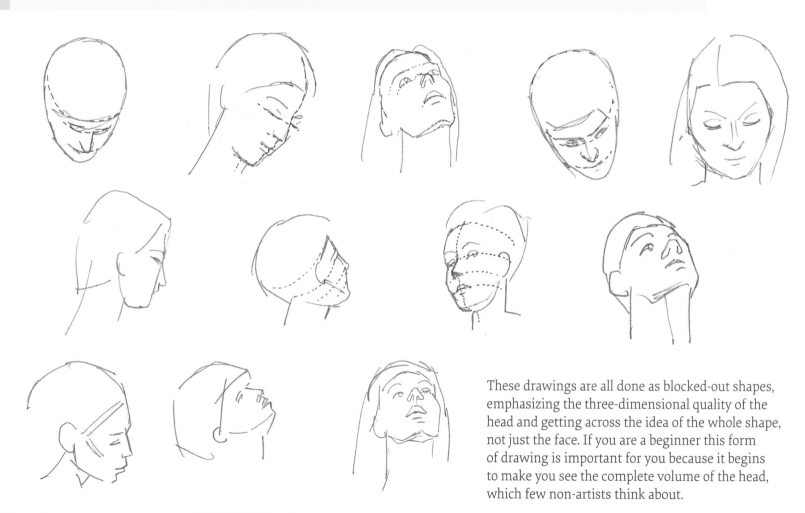

These drawings are all done as blocked-out shapes, emphasizing the three-dimensional quality of the head and getting across the idea of the whole shape, not just the face. If you are a beginner this form of drawing is important for you because it begins to make you see the complete volume of the head, which few non-artists think about.

These drawings show other versions of heads in different positions, but this time with the hair and features put in more naturally. Try to draw as many different versions of heads as you can, because it will improve your ability to draw portraits in more depth. Do as many of them from life as possible, resorting to photographs if need be. Notice how the shadows on the faces give an extra dimension, not only to the form but also to the expressions.

Facial Features

Here are the things to look for when you are making a preliminary study of the sitter's face before you start to draw it. It is these little details that are going to make the difference between the portrait looking like the sitter or not.

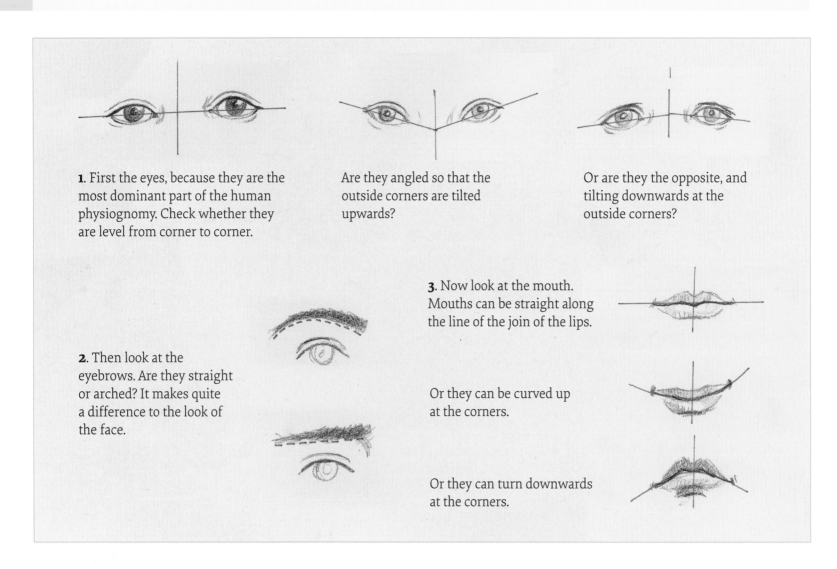

1. First the eyes, because they are the most dominant part of the human physiognomy. Check whether they are level from corner to corner.

Are they angled so that the outside corners are tilted upwards?

Or are they the opposite, and tilting downwards at the outside corners?

2. Then look at the eyebrows. Are they straight or arched? It makes quite a difference to the look of the face.

3. Now look at the mouth. Mouths can be straight along the line of the join of the lips.

Or they can be curved up at the corners.

Or they can turn downwards at the corners.

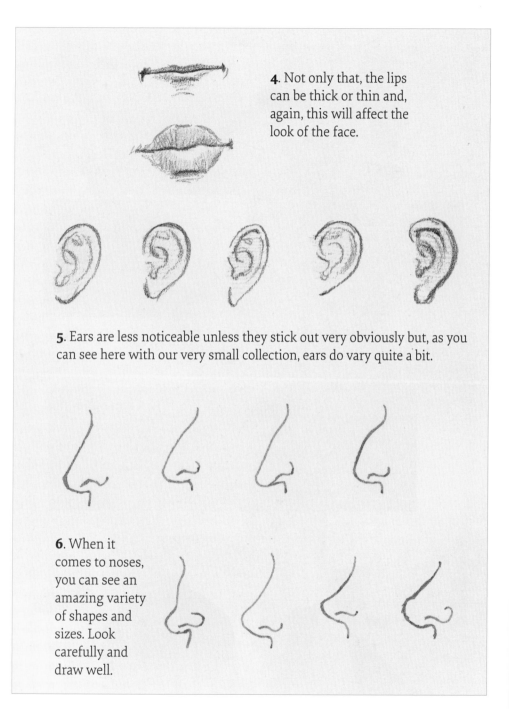

4. Not only that, the lips can be thick or thin and, again, this will affect the look of the face.

5. Ears are less noticeable unless they stick out very obviously but, as you can see here with our very small collection, ears do vary quite a bit.

6. When it comes to noses, you can see an amazing variety of shapes and sizes. Look carefully and draw well.

Artist's Note

When it comes to hair, the most obvious differences are in length and whether the hair is curly or straight. There is generally less range in style among men, though the advent of thinning hair with age does tend to change the look of someone's face. Shown here are just four examples of how to tackle short, straight, curly and long hair.

Features in More Detail

Now we will look at these features in closer detail and note some of the things you are sure to come across, if you learn to look carefully enough.

You will have noticed the formation of the average eye is not quite as you may have imagined before you began drawing the human face. The iris – that is, the coloured part – features quite large in the centre of the eye and yet is hardly ever seen completely. Normally, what you see is a part of the iris hidden under the top eyelid, and the bottom edge of the iris just touching the bottom lid.

1. The lower eyelid shows its thickness, whereas the thickness of the upper lid is usually hidden by the eyelashes.

2. Seen from the side, the shape of the eye changes dramatically, and is more obviously a ball held behind the lids. You can actually see the bulge of the lens on the front of the eyeball.

3. Then there are eyes with very heavy or drooping eyelids. In an older person, as here, the iris retreats further under the upper eyelid and does not quite touch the lower one.

4. In Oriental eyes the top lid is obscured altogether, which has the effect of simplifying the shape of the eye and, incidentally, making it smoother to draw.

5. Noses are much easier to draw in profile, as these examples show. When drawing from the front, ascertain the shape by observing the shadows cast by the projection. From these three examples, you will see that because it casts a larger shadow, the beaky or aquiline shape shows more clearly than either the retroussé or the straight nose.

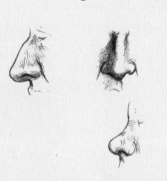

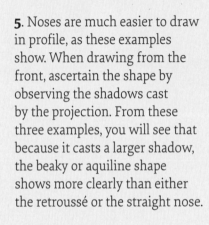

6. With mouths, the difference between the front and the profile view of them is radical. Seen from the front, all these lips are easy enough to draw, but from the side you begin to see that the most important part of the mouth is where it opens. It does mean that when you draw the mouth, that part where the two lips meet is all-important for giving the right effect to convince your viewer. With the smiling mouth the real problem is whether you should, or should not, emphasize the teeth. If you overdo it they can look quite grotesque, so go carefully.

Ears, foreheads and chins can show just as much variation as noses, mouths and eyes. Study them carefully and work on building up a good bank of them in your reference sketchbooks.

7. Here are some examples of ears from the front and side.

8. And there are examples of foreheads, too, which as you can see are just as varied, although it's a feature that doesn't immediately grasp your attention.

9. Finally, we have some examples of chins, seen from the side. Most chins are either in line with the forehead or slightly behind it. However, some project further forward than the forehead.

Mapping Out a Portrait

Once you have spent some time studying the proportions of the head and facial features, you are ready to tackle a portrait drawing. Starting out on a portrait is always a bit tricky, but there are time-honoured methods of approach that should help you.

Step 1

First, treat the head like any other object and make a rough sketch of the overall shape. This is not as easy as it sounds because the hair often hides the outline and so you may have to do a little bit of guesswork to get as close to the basic shape as you can.

Step 2

When you have done that, block in the hair area quite simply – not trying to make it look like hair – and note how much of the overall shape it occupies.

Step 3

Now comes the most critical part of the drawing, the features. These must be placed at the correct levels on the face, in a very simple form. Check by measuring if you are in any doubt, but remember that normally the eyes are halfway between the top of the head and the point of the chin, and make sure the eyes are far enough apart. Also, check the size of the nose and its relationship with the mouth. In this example, the face is seen three-quarters on, and this means that the space occupied by the far side of the face measures much less than the near side.

Step 4

Once you are happy with the position and shape of the features, you can erase any guidelines and start to draw them in greater detail. Take your time at this stage, as it is crucial in obtaining a likeness of your subject.

Step 5

Add in the main areas of shadow across the entire head and face, keeping the shading light to start with. On the hair, use marks that follow the direction of growth.

Step 6

Stand back from your drawing to assess it and make any corrections to the shading or features. If you are satisfied that all is correct, then you can finish off by refining both the shapes and the tonal areas, deepening the areas of shadow and picking out any highlights with an eraser.

An Alternative Approach

This alternative approach to drawing the head is one used by many portrait painters, and it works just as well as that shown on the previous pages.

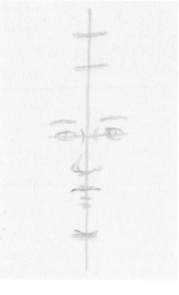

Step 1

First, you draw a vertical line to represent the length of the head from the top to the chin and then carefully mark on it the positions of the eyes, which should be halfway down.

Draw in – very simply – the shapes of the eyes in their relative positions.

A mark halfway between where the eyes are and the bottom mark, which is the chin, will give you the position of the nose. Draw it in as near as possible to the shape you can see.

The position of the mouth is to be marked in next, and here you will have to be more careful. Refer back to the head proportions on page 154 if you need to.

Step 2

The next part is very important. First draw in the shapes of the eyes, nose and mouth very carefully. Notice how, in this view of a slightly turned head, the far eye and the far side of the mouth are a little shorter than the near side.

Next draw in the eyebrows. Again the far eyebrow is shorter than the nearer one.

When you do the nose, the shadow side can be put in, too, because that helps to define the character of the nose more clearly. It is worth taking the trouble to get all these shapes right.

The next thing is to put in the ear that you can see from this point of view. Lengthwise, it is situated between the eyebrow at the top and the end of the nose at the bottom. Check the distance between the outside edge of the nearest eye and the front edge of the ear, relating its distance to that of the length of the nose.

Then draw in the point of the chin.

Step 3

Now complete the whole shape of the head, carefully observing the shapes. Add some shading to define the shape of the whole head and the neck area. Treat all the areas of shading fairly lightly at first.

Step 4

Finally, start to block in the darker tones, either with a graphite pencil, or with coloured pencils as in this example. If you are using colours, start with the lightest first and work over them with the darker colours. If you want the face to look brighter, give it a darker background colour.

Effects with Technique

There are various ways of producing an effective picture by varying the technique you use. Here are a few variations in the treatment of the head of a young man to show you some of the stylistic possibilities.

In this pencil rendition, the tones have been worked over with a drawing aid called a stump or a stub, which is just paper rolled up into a solid stump and sharpened at both ends. The stump has been used to smudge the pencil to produce a softer, more gradual tonal effect on the areas of shadow. This approach requires fairly vigorous handling of the pencil and the production of strong lines to ensure that the smudging is effective.

Two grades of pencil (B and 2B) have been used to create texture within the tone. The softer tonal areas, such as the background and hair, were achieved by means of a graphite pencil stick.

The method used here, in ink, is time-consuming. The tonal areas have been carefully built up with different kinds of cross-hatching and random strokes, giving a solid feel to the head and allowing an exploratory approach to the shape and form.

Using a brush and ink or watercolour in one colour will give a painterly feel to your portrait. When attempting this approach, don't be too exact with your brush-strokes. Build up the outlines with fairly loose strokes and then fill in the large areas of tone, initially with very pale washes and then with darker washes.

There has been no attempt to build up tone in this example in ink. Open and loosely drawn, it is a very rapid method requiring confidence and facility with the pen. You need to feel your way with your strokes and, as with the previous example, resist the temptation to be too precise.

Up to this point the examples given have been explorations of what you see. This next method is all about using technique to capture form, not likeness. For this approach the initial drawing of the shapes of the head and features has to be very accurate, otherwise the simplification and smoothing out that is the essence of this method will render the final result a bit too perfect in form. You may find that your first swift drawing has captured more of a likeness of the sitter than has your finished drawing. Once you have got the features and tonal areas down, you begin the technical exercise of making the outlines very smooth and continuous so there are no breaks in the line. Then, with a stump, work on the tonal areas until they graduate very smoothly across the surface and are as perfect in variation and as carefully outlined as it is possible to make them.

Drawing Your Family

You may wish to make more informal sketches of your family and friends, and it is of great benefit to draw the people you have easiest access to and whom you know very well. This in-depth knowledge can help to give your portraits more power.

I decided to have a go at drawing most of the members of my family who were in the house one Christmas, and I started with my grandchildren. Of course young children and babies will not sit still for you for long so this is probably an occasion when photography can come to your aid. It does help to have the originals around as well, though, because this helps to inform your drawings from photographs that you have taken yourself.

Next my granddaughter lounging on the floor, kicking her legs and giggling. Here, I concentrated on her gleeful expression.

Here is my youngest grandson, caught in his mother's arms and laughing at the camera. As you can see, his round, open eyes and nose and mouth are all set neatly in the centre of the rounded form of his head and face.

My eldest grandson, looking a bit shy but amused. He couldn't stay still for long, so I took a photograph just before I started drawing.

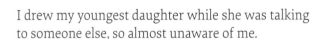

I drew my youngest daughter while she was talking to someone else, so almost unaware of me.

Then come drawings of my wife and my youngest son's girlfriend, both engaged in conversation with other people. Catching a fleeting expression is not easy, but with a little practice, you soon get it right.

Next my son-in-law grinning at the camera (left) and my youngest son about to go out (below). My son's hat helped to define the facial area rather neatly and give character to the drawing.

All these drawings of my family were done close together in time, often based on photographs that I took myself and informed by the people present at the gathering. It is an enjoyable and instructive exercise that is well worth doing.

The Human Figure: Proportions

Here we look at the proportions of the whole figure, which are important to understand even if you only draw clothed figures. As you can see from the illustrations shown here, the proportions of both male and female figures are similar vertically but they do differ slightly horizontally. The widest area of a man is usually his shoulders, whereas in a mature woman it is usually the hips. Generally, but by no means universally, the male is larger than the female and has a less delicate bone structure.

Not many people conform exactly to the classical ideal of proportion, but it is a reliable rough guide to help you draw the human figure. These proportions only work if the figure is standing straight with head held erect.

Classical proportion is worked out on the basis of the length of one head fitting into the full height of the body eight times, as you can see here. The halfway mark is the pubic edge of the pelvic structure, which is proportionally the same in males and females. The knees are about two head lengths from the centre point. When the arm is hanging down loosely the fingertips should be about one head length from the central point.

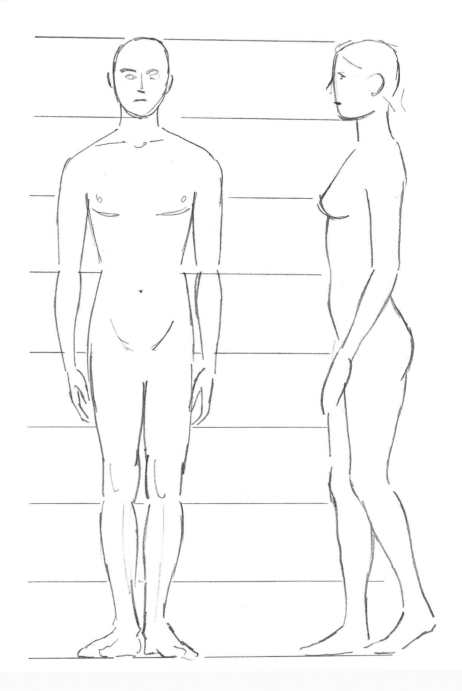

Proportions of Children

The proportions of children's bodies change very rapidly and because children grow at very different speeds what is true of one child at a certain age may not always be so true of another. Consequently, the drawings here can only give an average guide to children's changes in proportion as they get older.

    The thickness of children's limbs varies enormously but often the most obvious difference between a child, an adolescent and an adult is that the limbs and body become more slender as part of the growing process. In some types of figure there is a tendency towards puppy fat which makes a youngster look softer and rounder.

At the beginning of life the head is much larger in proportion to the rest of the body than it will be later on. Here I have drawn a child of about 18 months old, giving the sort of proportion you might find in a child of average growth. The height is only three and a half times the length of the head, which means that the proportions of the arms and legs are much smaller in comparison to those of an adult.

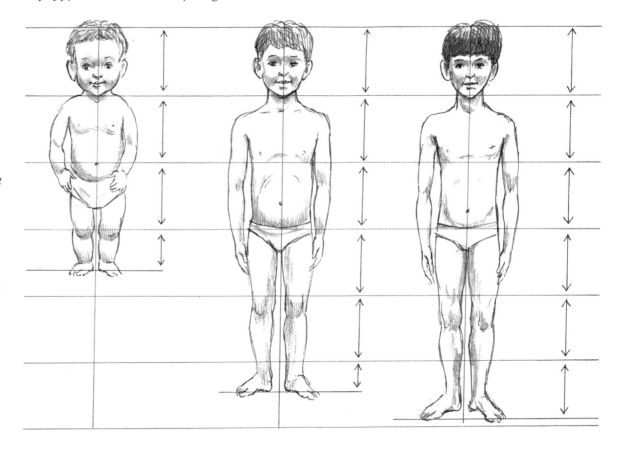

At the age of about six or seven, a child's height is a little over five times the length of the head, though again this is a bit variable. At about 12 years, the proportion is about six times the head size. Notice how in younger children the halfway point in the height of the body is much closer to the navel, but this gradually lowers until it reaches the adult proportion at the pubic edge of the pelvis where the legs divide.

Poses in Close-up

Here we begin to look at the figure and how the shape changes in different poses. You can explore this for yourself by getting someone to adopt different positions for you to study.

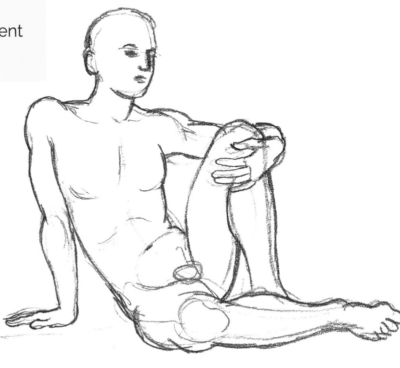

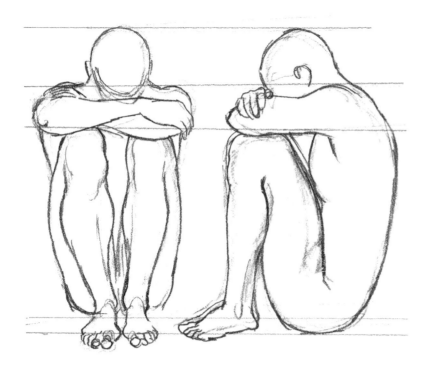

In this more relaxed pose the use of foreshortening is vital to the success of the drawing. Part of one leg and arm have been foreshortened to convey the effect of a limb pointing towards the viewer.

Look at this drawing of a man sitting curled up, his limbs folded to make a compact shape. Note the way you can measure the thighs and lower leg against each other and then measure both of these elements against the torso. See how the arms tuck into each other so neatly. I have added some guidelines to show the compactness of the pose.

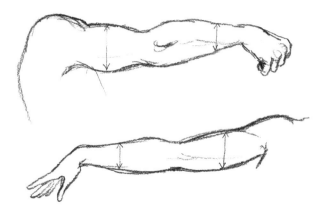

The upper arm is thicker than the lower arm or forearm. The wrist is the thinnest part of the arm and the furthest from the torso.

Artist's Note

Drawing the complete human body unclothed is really the subject of a life class. Generally speaking, the best you will be able to coax from friends and family is a pose in a bathing costume, since other than the young and beautiful most people are too self-conscious to subject themselves to such close scrutiny. This is sufficient for a general view of the body, but if you need to study it more closely in order to understand the bones and muscles showing on the surface a tutored course in life drawing is the obvious answer.

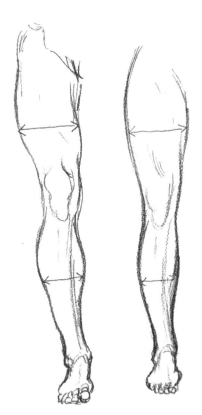

The leg below the knee is generally thinner than the leg above the knee. The thinnest part of the leg, the ankle, is furthest from the torso.

Pipe-cleaner arms and hose-like legs are common faults in the drawings of beginners. You can eradicate this problem by noting the variation in thickness of the limbs. The areas of the biceps, shoulders, thighs and calves are generally the fleshiest and most pronounced parts.

Studying Different Poses

Now try working from photographs or live models with a view to giving yourself experience of capturing different kinds of poses. If you can find good photographs of poses with some movement in them, use them first to trace and then to copy, keeping the original next to your drawing as reference.

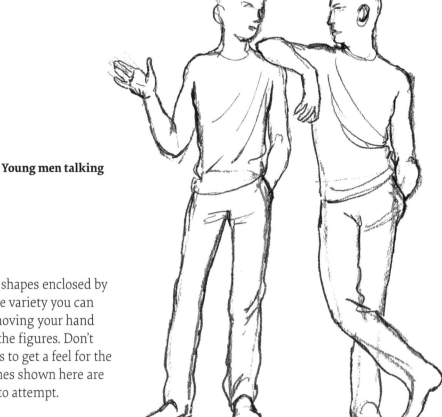

Young men talking

Get used to looking at the whole shape, including the shapes enclosed by the limbs, in order to see the general outline. The more variety you can get in these sorts of sketches the better. Get used to moving your hand quite fast, but observing closely the essential lines of the figures. Don't concern yourself with details as the important thing is to get a feel for the forms and proportions of the whole figure. The sketches shown here are to give you ideas of the types of poses you might like to attempt.

A girl relaxing, probably talking or watching a video

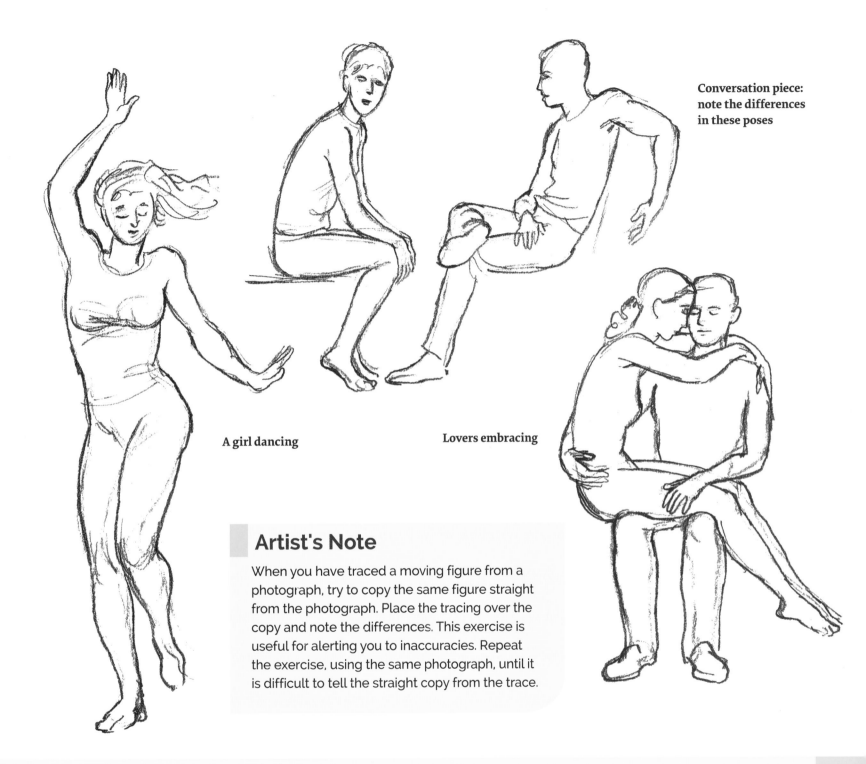

A girl dancing

Lovers embracing

Artist's Note

When you have traced a moving figure from a photograph, try to copy the same figure straight from the photograph. Place the tracing over the copy and note the differences. This exercise is useful for alerting you to inaccuracies. Repeat the exercise, using the same photograph, until it is difficult to tell the straight copy from the trace.

Form and Clothing

Drawing clothing requires some study in order to be clear about how materials behave and what happens when they are covering the body. The main purpose of these exercises is to teach you how folds work, which depends largely on the type of fabric.

Try drawing an arm in a sleeve or a leg in tracksuit bottoms and carefully note the main folds and how the bend in the arm or leg affects them. In sleeves, the wrinkles can take on an almost patterned look, like triangles and diamond shapes alternating.

Start by very simply putting in the main lines of the creases. Note how on the jacket the folds and creases appear shorter and sharper across the sleeve, whereas on the tracksuit they appear longer and softer down the length of the leg. Shade in where necessary to give the drawing substance.

The patterns on these sleeves look almost stylized, partly because the material is a bit stiff.

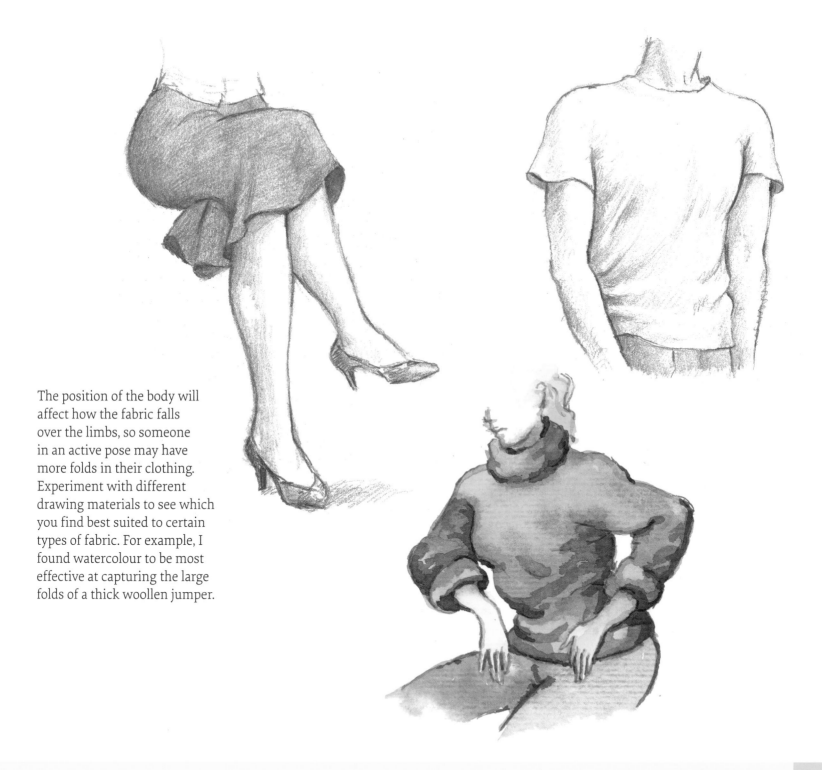

The position of the body will affect how the fabric falls over the limbs, so someone in an active pose may have more folds in their clothing. Experiment with different drawing materials to see which you find best suited to certain types of fabric. For example, I found watercolour to be most effective at capturing the large folds of a thick woollen jumper.

Portrait Poses

There's an infinite variety of poses that can be adopted for full-figure portraits, but eventually you have to rely on your sitter being able to adopt the position that you feel would be the best. Here I have suggested a few poses that might be used, but you will no doubt find many others.

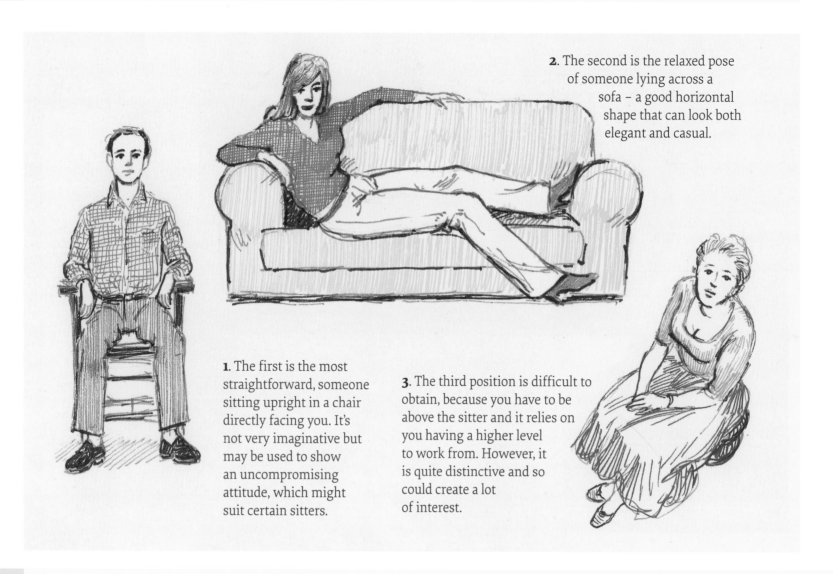

2. The second is the relaxed pose of someone lying across a sofa – a good horizontal shape that can look both elegant and casual.

1. The first is the most straightforward, someone sitting upright in a chair directly facing you. It's not very imaginative but may be used to show an uncompromising attitude, which might suit certain sitters.

3. The third position is difficult to obtain, because you have to be above the sitter and it relies on you having a higher level to work from. However, it is quite distinctive and so could create a lot of interest.

4. Next I show the sort of informal pose that anyone might take up. Such positions give a natural quality to the portrait.

5. The fifth one is much the easiest pose for the sitter to adopt, as long as you don't expect them to keep their arms above their head for too long.

6. This pose is rather stylised, reminiscent of those eighteenth- or nineteenth-century aristocratic figures.

7. This example shows one of the most natural positions for a portrait, where the sitter is dressed in their best clothes and enthroned in a chair – a sort of party piece.

8. (a) You might consider whether you want a rich decorative element to your portrait or, conversely, a very plain, unadorned image. This will depend on your sitter, and you have to try to match their personality with the way you portray them. **(b)** You might decide that you need a little drama in the pose of the sitter, as in this painting by James McNeill Whistler (1834–1903)

a

b

c

titled *Symphony in White, No. 2: The Little White Girl*, where the subject of the portrait is reflected in a mirror, standing by a mantelpiece. **(c)** Or you might want to refer to the particular abilities of your sitter, as in this example of a writer sitting at this desk.

A Full-Figure Portrait

Having considered the various poses on the previous pages, you can now attempt a portrait of someone who will be prepared to pose for you for a while. I took as my model my six-year-old grandson, who is not easy to keep in one position, but I put him in front of the television to watch a film that I knew would interest him so he sat for a little longer than usual. That in itself is a lesson – make your models comfortable and happy and you will get more time to draw them!

Step 2

The next stage is to put in all the shadows that seem relevant, again keeping everything simple – but it is at this stage that the face needs to become recognizable.

Step 1

At first you will need to draw the main shape of the figure. Keep it very simple to start with and use your eraser, correcting as much as you can at this stage – it saves time later on.

Step 3

Once you are sure everything is the right shape and in the correct proportion, begin to work into the picture to make it come to life. Take great care over the head and the features of the face, because this is where the picture becomes a portrait of a particular individual rather than of just anyone. Build up the tones in such a way as to stress the softness or hardness of the form.

A Figure Composition

For a composition in which groups of figures are central to the artist's statement, choose a scene with which you are familiar. I have decided on a jazz version of the dance hall or night club which, as a young man, I found endlessly fascinating, chiefly for the way people revealed themselves in terms of what they wore and how they moved. This is where people go to dance, show off, have fun and dress up to be seen, all at the same time.

Step 1

First, you need to decide on the number of figures, and how you want to portray them. I wanted to show three pairs dancing and three other individuals on the sidelines, so to speak. I decided to leave the actual venue rather vague, just a dark space with some strobe lights to suggest the activity.

My main couple, designed to occupy the centre of the picture, are a young man and woman dancing, standing separately from one another but holding each other by one hand.

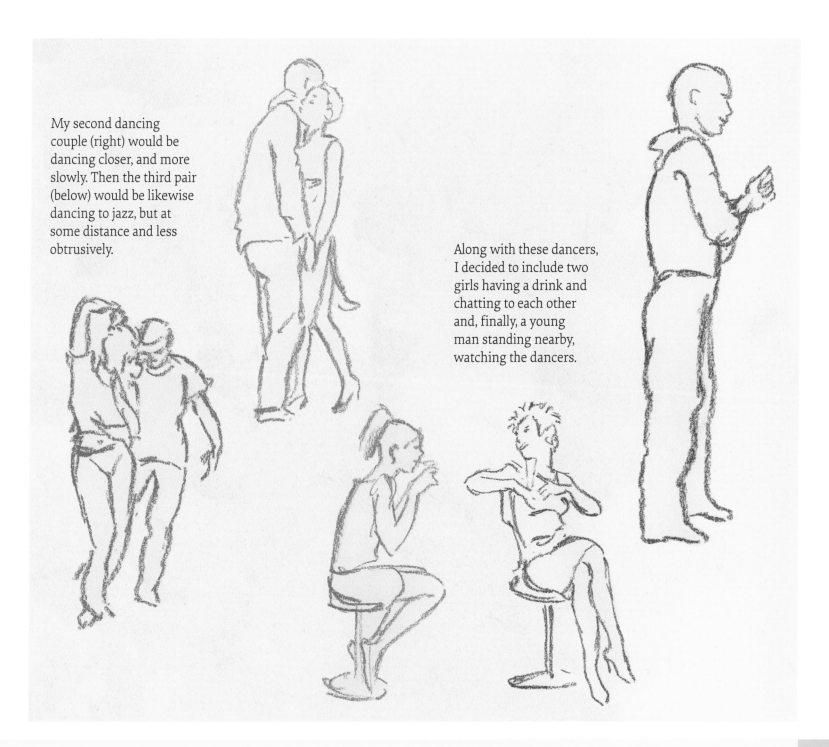

My second dancing couple (right) would be dancing closer, and more slowly. Then the third pair (below) would be likewise dancing to jazz, but at some distance and less obtrusively.

Along with these dancers, I decided to include two girls having a drink and chatting to each other and, finally, a young man standing nearby, watching the dancers.

Step 2

Having drawn these up, so that I had some idea of what they should look like, I then arranged them across the page, as though they were all in the scene together. I put the two girls in close and at one end. Behind them, I placed the solitary young man. Immediately next to them were the first pair of dancers and they took up most of the centre space. Visible behind them, slightly smaller, were the other two jazz dancers. Finally, I put the slow-dancing couple on the end.

Behind these main figures, I showed silhouettes of people in the far reaches of the club. Of course, if the club was any good it would be very crowded, but the silhouette technique is a form of artistic licence, as my task would be all the harder if I had to put in many more bodies.

Step 3

Using pastel as my medium, I decided to go for an atmospheric use of colour. So although I sketched in the local colour lightly to begin with, I allowed the tones of light and shade to dictate the colour values to me. In such a venue, anyway, the light would be very low, except for the strobe effects, which would dominate the scene.

I made the whole background dark with a few streaks of white, yellow and red breaking up the tone. On the dancers' figures, I made sure that there were yellow and light blue flicks of light around the edges, to indicate the reflection of the strobe flashes. The foreground figures were significantly lighter than the background. I also indicated some reflection on the floor under their feet, to give the impression of a smooth surface. The floor was a cool blue and the upper background was deep purple. None of the figures were drawn in any great detail because a looser mode of drawing suggests movement better.

Portraits after Master Artists

To finish this chapter on drawing people, we look at some examples of the changing ages of humanity as seen through the eyes of some of the great artists. These masters have conveyed the subtle signs of youth and age on the human face with tremendous skill.

The original of this portrait of a dreamy ten-year-old boy, by Antonella da Messina (c. 1430–79), was done in silverpoint, the precursor to pencils, which were not invented until the 16th century. I used a B pencil to recreate the closely grouped lines with a little cross-hatching on the face and very sharp, clear lines around the eyes and mouth and for the main strands of hair.

The portrait by Diego Velázquez (1599–1660) of the five-year-old Infanta of Spain captures the innocence of early childhood. Her sweet expression contrasts with the dark background and her stiff formal dress, accentuating her innocence. Soft black pencil (B) and graphite stick (2B) were used for this copy. With the exception of the edges of the eyes and the dress, the lines were kept sparse and light. The broad edge of the graphite produced the dusky background tones.

We happen to know that the sitter for this portrait by Jan Van Eyck (1390–1441), the Cardinal of Sante Croce, Florence, is fifty-six years old. The lines of the eyes, ears, nose, mouth and outline of the face are precise and give clear signs of the ageing process. The technique is generally smooth and light with some cross-hatching in the tonal areas. Although Van Eyck portrays his subject as still powerful, there is also a sense of resignation.

Rembrandt Van Rijn (1606–69) drew himself throughout his life, from early adulthood until just before his death, and has left us an amazing record of his ageing countenance. In this copy of a self-portrait done when he was about sixty years old, a smudgy technique with a soft 2B pencil was used in imitation of the chalk in the original.

A copy in chalk of a portrait of Edouard Vuillard's mother, done when she was in her eighties, describes age in a most economic way. Echoing the original, I was sparing with the tone and detail, and allowed the wavering lines to follow the gentle disintegration of the flesh on the face.

In these examples after master artists, the faces of the individual people are less important than their clothing and the settings where they are shown, which in both cases reflect their social status.

This drawing is made after a famous painting by Thomas Gainsborough (1727–88) called *Mr and Mrs Andrews*. Mr Andrews was a landowner, and the painting shows the couple in a countryside setting, on their own land. They are set to one side of the composition, leaving plenty of space for the idyllic scenery; the fields and the livestock that belong to them. Placing the figures at a vantage point, with their elegant clothes and confident stance, Gainsborough's portrait is a clear depiction of their wealthy social status.

In this drawing of *Mowing Bracken* after a painting by Henry Herbert La Thangue (1859–1929) the focus is not on the individual shown, but on the traditional job he is doing and the rural setting. The labourer's face is turned down and away from the viewer so that his features are barely visible. This is a depiction of a way of life, rather than an individual.

Chapter Seven

NATURE AND LANDSCAPES

This section is all about getting to grips with elements of the natural world and the composition of a landscape. We shall start with a brief look at animals, as they are a subject apart; then we shall move on to look at the components of a landscape, from grass, plants and trees to water, rocks and sky.

Looking through a frame made from a piece of card will help you select a manageable composition from an expanse of landscape, which can be confusing at first. There are many ways of approaching a landscape, and your own particular view is part of the interest that your drawing will create. Expanses of calm or turbulent water, large trees and rock formations all bring extra power to your drawing, so make the most of any unusual landscape you come across – but don't feel deterred by more mundane terrain, as the way you handle it can equally catch the viewer's eye.

You may be lucky enough to have an enchanting rural scene close by, but if not there will probably be a local park or nature reserve that will stand in for a bigger view. However, if this is the case it won't be long before you want to make a journey to more open countryside, and you will need to make sure you are well-equipped. Arm yourself with plenty of well-sharpened pencils so that you do not have to keep sharpening your only one. A really good hard-backed sketchbook is also a good investment for working outdoors.

Animals

Drawing animals is not unlike drawing humans in that you will find yourself dealing with the same issues of getting proportions and shapes correct. The major difference, of course, is that many animals won't stay still long enough for you to manage more than a quick sketch. This is where photography can come to your aid, especially for supplementing swift sketches done at the same time.

I took a chance that our cat, who had curled up on a cushion, wasn't going to move unless somebody disturbed him. Initially he seemed to be just a furry shape with a couple of ears poking out, but as I began to draw I saw more of the curves of his legs and body under the long fur and the patches of white fur acted as useful definition points.

To draw a cat moving I had to rely on my memory, and because I've observed them a lot it wasn't difficult to make a simple drawing of a cat playing with a ball of paper, tail held high. As I'd decided it was a black cat there was no detail to draw – just a dark silhouette, getting the movement as close as possible to how I remembered it.

Drawing a dog while it is asleep gives you a chance to complete your drawing before it moves, but to catch a characterful face and attitude that makes for a really attractive picture of a dog you may find it easiest to work from photographs. For this image, I lightly sketched the main shapes of the dog before working over the whole picture to build up an impression of fur and gleaming eyes and nose. To describe the fur texture, I made pencil marks in the direction that the hair grows, which varies over the whole body of the dog.

You may have a farm near you that opens to the public, which will give you an ideal opportunity to draw some domestic farm animals; otherwise you'll probably be able to find cows and sheep in fields not too far away. Of course the animals won't keep still, but they won't be moving about very rapidly unless they're alarmed. This gives you a chance to sketch some quick drawings. Sometimes just watch the animals closely without drawing, and notice how they move repeatedly into the same positions – unlike humans, or indeed cats, they are not mobile in an extravagant way. When you have observed them for a while, start drawing and try to catch them in the positions they seem to favour most. As you can see, I tend to achieve lots of bits and pieces instead of detailed drawings.

A Garden Bird

Many of us like to watch the birds in our gardens, but they are rarely still for more than a few seconds so when it comes to drawing them, you may find a good photograph helpful. Try making some sketches of live birds first, to get the feel of their brisk movements and alert postures.

Step 1

Make a careful line drawing of your chosen bird, paying attention to the detail of the main shapes. The legs are barely wider than the thickness of the pastel line, contrasting with the rounded body and head. Include the branch or bird table where your bird is perched.

Step 2

Block in the main areas of colour quite lightly with your pastel or other chosen medium. Identify areas of shadow and mark them in.

Step 3

Start to give your image a lift by adding the darkest area of tone, particularly around the underside of the robin's tail feathers and his beady eye. Additional touches of yellow, orange and even purple will add richness to his red breast.

Step 4

Work over the whole bird in some detail to give a convincing effect of its feathery body. Use a stump to blend the colours and create a smooth sheen, before adding more dashed marks in the direction of the feathers. The inside of the robin's open mouth should be very dark, with thin highlights along the edges of its beak where it catches the light.

Choosing a Landscape

Finding a landscape to draw can be very time-consuming. Some days I have spent more time searching than drawing. Never regard search time as wasted as you will learn something new on every outing. Here we look at a few useful tips for choosing a view and getting the basics down on paper.

A view along a diminishing perspective, such as a road, river, hedge or avenue, or even along a ditch, almost always allows an effective result. The change of size gives depth and makes such landscapes very attractive. Well-drawn examples of this type suggest that we, the onlookers, can somehow walk into them. See pages 220–1 for some examples.

A landscape seen from a high point is usually eye-catching, although not always easy to draw. Look for a high point that offers views across a valley to other high points in the distance. From such a perspective the landscape is somehow revealed to the viewer. If you try this approach, you will have to carefully judge the sizes of buildings, trees and hillsides to ensure the effect of distance is recognized in your picture.

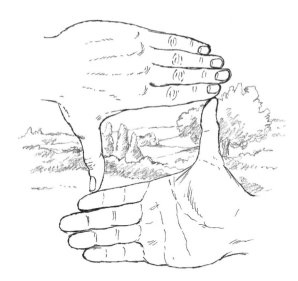

The hands can be used to isolate and frame a chosen scene to help you decide how much landscape to include.

A card frame can be used instead of the hands.

Once a scene is chosen, the main areas are drawn very simply. Noting where the eye level or horizon appears in the picture is very important. Attending to these basics makes it much easier to draw in the detail later.

Leaves, Grass and Flowers

Plants carefully drawn instantly tell us that they are very close to the viewer and help to impart a sense of depth and space to a scene, especially when you contrast the detail of the leaves with the more general structure of whole trees further away.

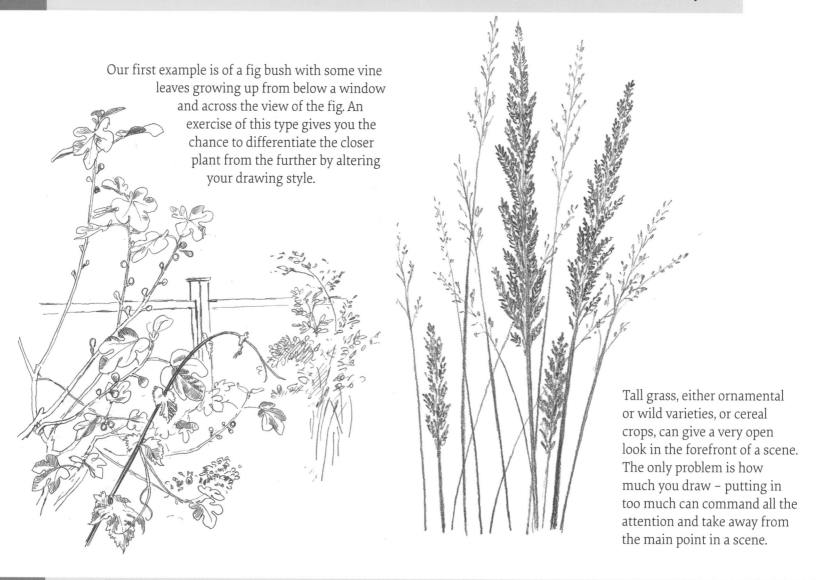

Our first example is of a fig bush with some vine leaves growing up from below a window and across the view of the fig. An exercise of this type gives you the chance to differentiate the closer plant from the further by altering your drawing style.

Tall grass, either ornamental or wild varieties, or cereal crops, can give a very open look in the forefront of a scene. The only problem is how much you draw – putting in too much can command all the attention and take away from the main point in a scene.

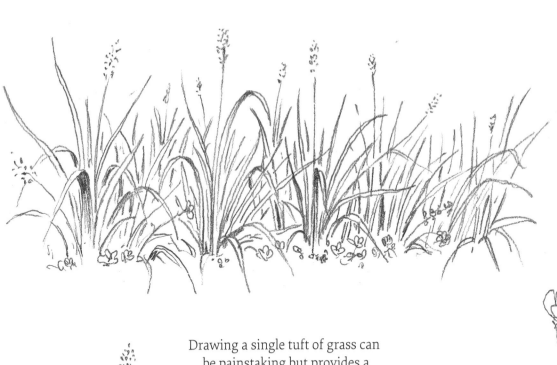

When you draw larger amounts of grass, note the overlapping tufts and smaller plants like clover tucked in at their bases.

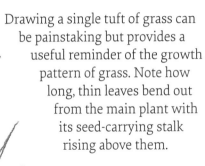

Drawing a single tuft of grass can be painstaking but provides a useful reminder of the growth pattern of grass. Note how long, thin leaves bend out from the main plant with its seed-carrying stalk rising above them.

A few clumps of flowers placed towards the front of a scene can quickly engage the eye and add to the freshness of your picture. Whatever variety of flower you choose, make sure you observe them closely to capture their habit and principal characteristics accurately.

Trees

Drawing trees can be a bit daunting because there seems to be so much to them. As we saw in Chapter 2 (see pages 50–1), you should begin with the overall shape and add areas of light and shade to denote the masses of leaves. When it comes to drawing deciduous trees in winter, close observation of their structure and the texture of bark will inform your landscape drawings.

Look for trees that will enable you to have a go at using the pencil to capture an indented and detailed outline, as here. You can add some textural marks to give the effect of leaves, particularly in the shady areas. Also make sure that some of the large branches are visible across the spaces within the main shape of the tree.

Notice the soft, almost cloud-like outline given to the groups of foliage in this example after Titian (c. 1488/90–1576) drawn in pen, ink and chalk. No individual leaves are actually shown. Smudges and lines of tone make patches of light which give an impression of thick bunches of leaves. The branches snake into the bulging form, disappearing where the foliage looks most dense.

Let us now take this further and look at some examples of trees with no foliage. The drawing on the right shows an old tree trunk, seen in close-up from below. It almost ceases to be a tree, becoming instead a vast, mysterious pillar with a small cavern halfway up. Notice how textured the trunk is, with multiple crevasses and a big hole where the bark has been split and the interior of the tree is revealed. It's a very powerful experience of rugged surfaces and dark hollows.

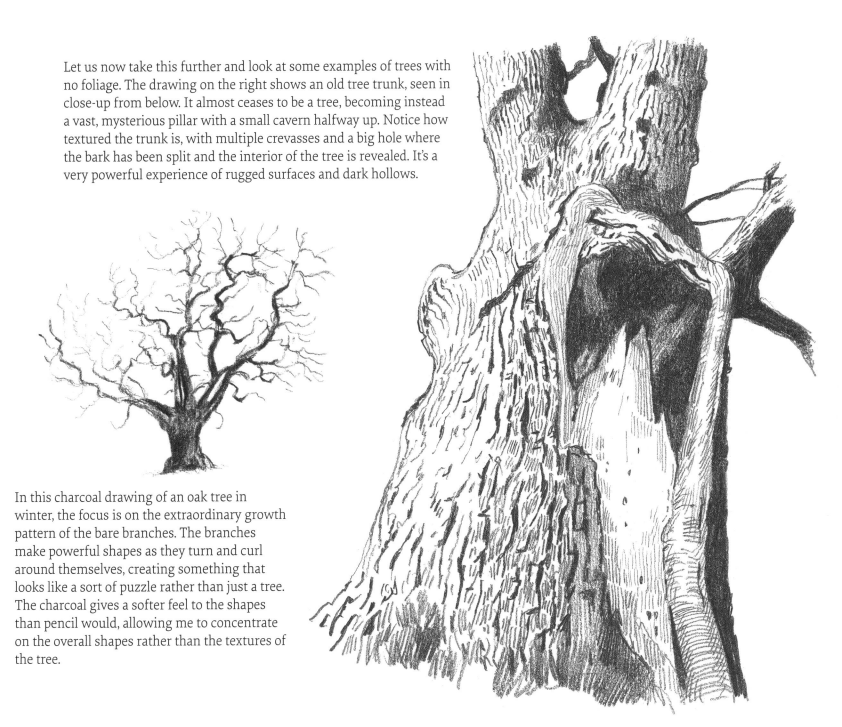

In this charcoal drawing of an oak tree in winter, the focus is on the extraordinary growth pattern of the bare branches. The branches make powerful shapes as they turn and curl around themselves, creating something that looks like a sort of puzzle rather than just a tree. The charcoal gives a softer feel to the shapes than pencil would, allowing me to concentrate on the overall shapes rather than the textures of the tree.

Grass and Trees in the Landscape

Grass and trees are two of the most fundamental elements in landscape. Once you have spent some time studying them, consider how they might be used as features in a landscape.

Tufts and hummocks of grass mingle with flowers in this close-up of a hillside. The foreground detail helps to add interest to the otherwise fairly uniform texture. The smoothness of the distant hills suggests that they too are grassy. The dark area of trees just beyond the edge of the nearest hill contrasts nicely with the fairly empty background.

Cultivated crops produce a much smoother top surface as they recede into the distance than do wild grasses. The most important task for an artist drawing this kind of scene is to define the height of the crop – here it is wheat – by showing the point where the ears of corn weigh down the tall stalks. The texture can be simplified and generalized after a couple of rows.

In this copy after John Constable (1776–1837) the trees are standing almost in silhouette against a bright sky with dark shadowy ground beneath them. The leaves are shown clumped together in dark masses to give the characteristic shapes of the trees.

The trees in this old orchard were heavy with foliage when I drew them, on a brilliant, sunny day. Nowhere here is there a suggestion of individual leaves, just broad soft shapes suggesting the bulk of the trees. They presented themselves as textured patches of dark and light with a few branches and their trunks outlined against this slightly fuzzy backdrop. An area of shadow under the nearest trees helps define their position on the ground. In the immediate foreground the texture of the tufts of grass helps to give a sense of space in front of the trees.

Water

Water in a landscape always adds an extra dimension to a drawing, reflecting the sky and the scenery and bringing light into your work. You may be lucky enough to live near the sea, but a river or lake will be just as interesting for your studies of water.

Water that's fairly still has large areas where nothing much is happening, making it an easier prospect. However, you will still have to be very careful and patient in making your drawing work well. In the drawing below, the river bank in the background gives a hard edge to all the water. There's a large area of dark tone across one side of the drawing that is actually caused by a couple of trees on the far bank, though they're not visible here. The major ripples are caused by a couple of ducks that have swum out of view. When you're drawing ripples like this make the dark parts quite strong, with areas of white paper breaking them up. A succession of horizontal marks going backwards and forwards across the surface gives an effect of ripples in the water. You can leave a large area of untouched paper to give the effect of the sun lighting up the surface of the stream.

The first picture (above) is a view of the sea with choppy-looking waves. To draw the sea you need a lot of patience, because of course it never stops moving. It's worth taking some photographs and then making a careful copy of one of them for practice before you try to draw from life. You need to keep making marks that give the same effect as the waves, but don't be too concerned if they don't all look exactly like the sea – just keep looking and drawing until you begin to get the feel of how the waves form and what you can see. Make sure that the waves closer to you are larger and further apart than the more distant ones; as your drawing gets to the horizon the waves are just tiny marks that create a texture of grey water in the distance. It's often a good idea to put a strip of the shore at the base of the picture to give the sense of where you are standing.

In this scene the water is in rapid movement, reflecting the light from the sky above. The surrounding scenery is the side of a rocky hill and the stream flows down to a pool at the base of the picture. There is not much sky as the depth of the hillside needs to be shown, and there is little vegetation except for grass. It is in effect a portrait of a waterfall. Most of the water is the white of the paper, with some judicious pencil marks to indicate how it flows over the steep rocks and into the swirling eddies below.

Artist's Note

You need time to capture accurately the swirls and shifting reflections in moving water. Leonardo da Vinci is said to have spent many hours just watching the movement of water, from running taps to torrents and downpours, in order to be able to draw the myriad shapes and qualities which such features present.

Reflections in Water

Water can give the landscape an added dimension of space, rather as the sky does. The fact that water is reflective always adds extra depth to a scene. The drawing of reflections is not difficult where you have a vast expanse of water flanked by major features with simple outlines, as in our main example here. Use the technique shown, which is a simple reversal, and you will find it even easier.

Here the water reflects the mountains and therefore gives an effect of expanse and depth as our eyes glide across it to the hills. The reflection is so clear because of the stillness of the lake (Wastwater in the English Lake District), and the hills being lit from one side. Only the ripples tell us this is water.

The mountains were drawn first and the water merely indicated. The drawing of the reflection was done afterwards, by tracing off the mountains and redrawing them reversed in the area of the water (see inset). This simple trick ensures that your reflection matches the shape of the landscape being reflected, but is only really easy if the landscape is fairly simple in feature. The ripple effect was indicated along the edges of each dark reflection, leaving a few white spaces where the distant water was obviously choppier and catching the sun.

How to draw in a reflection using a tracing technique.

This view of a pond after Claude Monet (1840–1926) is seen fairly close-up, looking across the water to trees and shrubs in the background. The light and dark tones of these reflect in the still water. Clumps of lily pads, appearing like small elliptical rafts floating on the surface of the pond, break up the reflections of the trees. The juxtaposition of these reflections with the lily pads adds another dimension, making us aware of the surface of the water as it recedes from us. The perspective of the groups of lily pads also helps to give depth to the picture.

The Sea

When you want to produce a landscape with the sea as part of it, you have to decide how much or little of the sea you want to show. The viewpoint you choose will determine whether you draw very little sea, a lot of sea, or all sea. In these examples we look at ways of viewing the sea in proportion to the land.

In this view of the Norfolk coast the sea takes up about one-eighth of the whole picture. Because the landscape is fairly flat and the sky is not particularly dramatic, the wide strip of sea serves as the far-distant horizon line. The result is an effective use of sea as an adjunct to depth in a picture. The calm sea provides a harmonious feel to the whole landscape.

In the next scene the sea takes up two-thirds of the drawing, with sky and land relegated in importance. The effect is one of stillness and calm, with none of the high drama often associated with the sea. The high viewpoint also helps to create a sense of detachment from everyday concerns.

When the sea is the whole landscape the result is called a seascape. The boat with the three fishermen is just a device to give us some idea of the breadth and depth of the sea. If the sea is to be the whole scope of your picture, a feature like this is necessary to give it scale.

Rocky Landscapes

Now we turn to the rock formations that help form the bone structure of the landscape. Stones, cliffs and rock formations often look quite dramatic, and a dramatic landscape is always a good spur to making a drawing. You can emphasize the power of the scene by using strong tonal contrasts and angled viewpoints.

This close-up of a rocky promontory shows starkly against a background of mountaintops drawn quite simply across the horizon. The rock wall effectively shadows the left-hand side of the hill, creating a strong definite shape. In the middleground, large boulders appear embedded in the slope. Smaller rocks are strewn all around. Note how the shapes of the rocks and the outline of the hill are defined by intelligent use of tone.

The main feature in this landscape is the stretch of rocky shoreline, its contrasting shapes pounded smooth by heavy seas. Pools of water reflect the sky, giving lighter tonal areas to contrast with the darker shapes of the rock. This sort of view provides a good example of aerial perspective: include more detail close to the viewer, less detail further away.

In this incredibly dramatic landscape, the jagged peaks of the mountain range in the background show rocks at their most awe-inspiring. The harsh tonal contrasts of the rocky outcrops contribute to the sense of an inhospitable landscape where little flora and fauna will survive. By contrast, the gently rolling foothills in the foreground of the picture show a more welcoming environment and are covered in vegetation. Here, the tonal contrasts are reduced to some light shading to show the shapes of the hills. In the centre ground is an area of higher hills, which start to take on the appearance of mountains, with their sharper silhouettes and deeper shadows. Using coloured pencils, I indicated these three areas of the landscape using different colours for each: predominantly green and brown colours in the foreground, a mix of purple and grey in the middleground and dark grey, white and yellow for the peaks themselves.

Clouds

The importance of clouds to suggest atmosphere and time in a landscape has been well understood by the great masters of art since at least the Renaissance period. When landscapes became popular, artists began to experiment with their handling of many associated features, including different types of skies.

The great landscape artists filled their sketchbooks with studies of skies in different moods. Clouded skies became a significant part of landscape composition with great care going into their creation, as the following range of examples shows.

After Caspar David Friedrich (1774–1840)
One of the leading German Romantic artists, Friedrich gave great importance to the handling of weather, clouds and light in his works. The original of this example was specifically drawn to show how the light at evening appears in a cloudy sky.

After a follower of Claude Lorrain (c. 1600–82)
This study is one of many such examples which show the care that artists lavished on this potentially most evocative of landscape features, with sunlight providing the backdrop to an elegantly shaped dark cloud.

After Willem van de Velde II (1633–1707)
Some studies were of interest to scientists as well as artists and formed part of the drive to classify and accurately describe natural phenomena.

After Alexander Cozens (1717–86)
The cloud effects are the principal interest here. The three evident layers of cloud produce an effect of depth, and the main cumulus on the horizon creates an effect of almost solid mass.

After J. M. W. Turner (1775–1851)
Together with many other English and American painters, Turner was a master of using cloud studies to build up brilliantly elemental landscape scenes. Note the marvellous swirling movement of the vapours, which Turner used time and again in his great land- and seascapes.

A Landscape with Clouds

In this composition in watercolour, clouds form the main feature of the overall landscape. Their shapes tower over the landscape of rolling hills and lake. Watercolour is a good medium for panoramic views like this, as you can cover the main areas quickly and effectively with your wash, not getting bogged down in the details of the landscape.

Step 1

Using a pencil, outline the main colour areas of your scene, starting with the line of the horizon. Make sure you place the horizon low enough to leave you more than half of your paper for the sky. Try to get the main shapes of the lake, hills and clouds as accurate as you can at this stage, but don't be afraid to simplify; I have included only five main areas of colour for my image (the lake, the hills, two bands of cloud, and the sky above).

Step 2

Using a light blue wash, fill the top area of sky and the lake area at the bottom of the image, following your outline shapes as closely as possible. Wash your brush thoroughly or use another before adding a yellow wash to the lower band of cloud, fading from the top.

Step 3

Fill the remaining colour areas with a green wash for the hills and purple for the higher band of clouds; these are the more threatening cumulus clouds. Where the hills meet the water, your green wash should be slightly darker to denote the shadowed edges of the lake.

Step 4

To finish your painting, add some nuance to all of your colour areas. For the lake, this is a light yellow wash where the clouds are reflected in the water. For the hills, some brown brings the closer hills into relief. For the bands of cloud, a light grey can be used to fade off the brighter colours and harmonize the overall look. The most care should be taken along the outlines of each area, where adding a darker wash will give a more dramatic effect. Take care not to overload your brush with these final additions as you don't want to overwork your image or cause the paper to buckle.

Garden Landscapes

The tamed landscape of a garden can sometimes seem a rather limiting space for the artist. However, if a garden has been designed with some flair, you will notice that the division of spaces in it creates a new proportion of landscape. This may be smaller but it can be just as interesting to draw as a more open, spacious view.

In these three examples, the gardeners have brought a clever aesthetic quality to the manipulation of plants, walls, hedges and so on, which is very rewarding to draw.

Here the hedges and bushes have been carefully trimmed to produce edges to pathways and more open spaces. The effect created is of an enclosed paradise garden. Seen from under an overhanging vine, the formal bushes clipped into large cushions define a route towards the end of an old wall, behind which stand tall clipped hedges.

Planted among all this formality are clumps of flowers, potted plants, bushes and places to sit. Rather like a beautiful room without a roof, it offers the artist options for drawing from many angles.

One of the main features to catch the eye here is the topiary, which appears like chess pieces set out in rows around a lawn with larger trees seen behind and a terrace with steps leading up to it. More formal than the first example, the garden is carefully contrasted against the larger trees gathered around in the background. The total effect is of a sort of natural sculpture.

In both of these drawings, the rows of clipped bushes give a good effect of perspective and make the space look larger than it is.

We go from the careful arrangements of the first two examples to a garden that looks like a mini-wilderness. The view I have chosen gives the impression of a wooded glade that somehow has managed to have a bridge built in it. The garden has been carefully designed to look both natural and attractive, with the Japanese moon-bridge creating a stylish reflection in the lake.

Leading the Eye into the Picture

The next three pictures show examples of scenes where a path or waterway draws the eye into the scene by leading away from the foreground into the distance. This very effective device is often used by artists to add interest to a picture.

In this view of the Chianti countryside in Italy a path winds across the scene past the open vineyards and a farm, disappearing into the hills. Nearly all the main features are on the right side of the picture, but they create a horizontal thrust across the scene, counter to the direction of the path.

The next scene is from Venice, Italy – a canal on the island of Burano with boats cluttering the edges of the water and a church tower looming up in the distance. We appear to be looking along the canal and the row of houses alongside it.

This watercolour by Peter de Wint (1784–1839) shows a lane dipping past a farmhouse in the Warwickshire countryside in England, where the view seems to be from the top of a slope. The large clumps of trees frame the whole picture in a satisfying way.

The Artist's Eye

We can learn a great deal from the compositions of professional photographers and painters and how they 'see' landscape. Here are examples of different kinds of landscapes; two of the drawings are taken from photographs and the other two from paintings.

This marvellous open sweep of mountainous landscape shows the valley of Glencoe in the Scottish Highlands. The original photograph catches the effect of sunlight and cloud shadows flitting across the land. The drawing reflects this by showing one side of the valley much more clearly. The side with the sharper perspective has one large bluff or spur in the shadow of the cloud, which helps to create depth and drama. A sense of scale is given by the road seen winding across the width of the valley and the minute cottage in the distance.

The second photograph-based scene is quite different, with a very localized view. Here we are close to trees and bushes viewed across an expanse of long grass and cow parsley. There is no distance to speak of and the interest lies in the rather cosy effect of a flattened path through the long grass, turning off suddenly with the luxuriant vegetation of summer hemming in the view. The effect is of a very English agricultural landscape; pleasant but without drama.

This beautiful sweep of landscape (after Corot, 1796–1875) is set in the Haute Savoie. The scope of the viewpoint is broad and shows mountain ranges in the distance. Closer up we see slopes and large trees in full foliage with, in the foreground, a large empty slope of grass, scrub and ploughed land. The broad movement from the high left towards the lower right side of the picture is balanced by the large group of trees at left of centre.

A view of Venice (after Monet) which combines compactness with a great effect of depth, thanks to the masterly handling of foreground details and distant buildings. Close up we see water and mooring poles rising out of the ripples to the left. Across the centre and right background, looking through mist, are the domes of Venetian churches caught in the light of the setting sun.

Colour as Emphasis

When a painter wants to make a strong emphasis in his or her composition, it is often the colour that brings out the point being made. Both these examples use colour to great effect and you can try out your own versions.

Monet is one of the great colourists of all time and he wasn't afraid to lay on the colour with abandon, producing work such as this sunset over the church of San Giorgio Maggiore in Venice (my version is above). This is a pretty dramatic sight at any time but when it is blazing with the colours of the setting sun it really becomes almost overstated. How can you do your own version of this sort of sight? Well, to start with you don't need to rush off to Venice; you can look around your own area for a building that is reflected in a river or lake, or the sea if you live near it. You will need a view that is towards the west to get the benefit of the next good sunset, so you will need to do a little bit of research of the locality. As an artist this is always valuable, so it is not time wasted.

Wassily Kandinsky (1866–1944) was not only a confirmed colourist but he also wanted to try to produce paintings that, like music, stood alone without a story. He painted this example of a landscape with boats in the autumn of 1908, and made the most of the colourful show put on by the trees. Not only that, but the light shining on the water and the boats is given its most lurid range of colour possible.

To get this sort of picture you would have to be prepared to throw out any ideas that you might have about tastefulness or restraint in visual terms. You will be able to find these colours in a scene but rarely with this intensity. So you will need to look hard at the possible picture you can get from a scene, picking one that allows you to go to town a bit with your range of colour.

A Landscape Project

Over the next pages I have shown how you might approach your own landscape composition, by first exploring an area and then choosing a view to develop. I decided to explore Hampton Court by the River Thames, close to where I used to live as a boy.

This area is not rural wilderness, but the kind of open parkland that many of us have within striking distance of home. Although there are plenty of houses in the vicinity, they are all well hidden by trees and the areas of footpath along the river. Also close by is a rather nice park that I used to play in when I was young, which is nicely wooded and has a small lake in it.

Preliminary sketches

First I walked around the park and the river to get ideas for my drawing. In the park I sketched very quickly this possible scene of the lake, which seemed nice and open.

Then I walked along the riverbank, making these three rough sketches of places I might choose to draw. As well as the sketches, I took several photographs of all the possible places that seemed attractive to me.

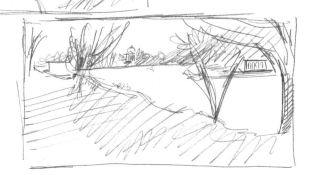

Looking at my sketches, I tried to decide which scene I was going to draw up more carefully. I returned to the park and began this view of the lake, with the rippling water and the willow trees around it.

As you can see I produced a fairly complete drawing, but somehow I was not quite satisfied with the result. You will find this often happens, which doesn't necessarily mean that there is anything wrong with your drawing – you are often the harshest critic of your work and you cannot be truly objective about it until much later on.

Step 1

I was keen to try something else, and so I went back to the riverbank and walked until I reached a spot that I had both sketched and photographed. I made another sketch, taking a bit more time over it than before.

Step 2

Satisfied that this was the place I wanted to draw, I then sat down and began to draw more carefully a simple outline drawing of the scene, making sure that all the trees were correctly aligned, and that the edges of the river were clearly marked. It had been raining, so there were many large puddles along the river path.

Step 3

Then I began to put in the tones that were evident, as well as textures, especially of the tree bark and the longer grass. I tried to keep this as even in tone as I could so that I would be able to see where the heavier and darker marks were going to be put later.

Step 4

Finally I worked up the drawing so that all the very dark tones and heavier textures would play their part in the balance of the composition. At this point the reflections in the puddles had to be carefully shown as well as the ripples on the river as it flowed past. Because by this time the sun was in the west, a lot of the trees were almost silhouettes, which helped to define the edge of the river and the trees in the distance. This seemed to me a more interesting drawing than the previous one (page 227) because there is more drama in the arrangement of the bare trees.

Chapter Eight

URBAN SCENES

The challenge with drawing urban scenes is that there's so much competing for your attention it can be difficult to make a sensible choice of subject. However, the same rules apply as in a rural landscape – select how much you are going to draw from your chosen viewpoint, and don't be confused by a lot of detail.

What you'll discover in the urban environment is that there are lots of incidental bits of architecture that seem to demand that you put them all in. However, this is where you have to decide exactly how much of this detail will be drawn precisely and how much will be reduced to very simple marks that just suggest the detail. Features such as windows, doors and chimneys are the obvious elements that come into this category. Most of what you see is recorded in your mind only as a general impression, and this is probably the best way to show it. The details that you do have to be precise about are those that are in the foreground or are points of focus.

The use of perspective depth is particularly important in drawing urban scenes, where the majority of elements in your drawing will have straight lines receding from your viewpoint. We will revisit the techniques of perspective and look at how to apply them to urban vistas, as well as considering how master artists have made city views into compelling works of art.

Street Scenes

Looking at the urban scene presents a different problem to the rural landscape because your view will often be cluttered with multiple signage, cars and so forth. For this reason, if you live in a quiet residential area it's a good idea to progress gradually from there to the centre of the town.

This drawing is a view down a road with the houses on the opposite side jumbled together and the pollarded tree at the side of the road acting like a frame on the left of the picture. The cars alongside the kerb are significantly cutting off your view of the road, which is the largest space in the scene. You immediately see how this lacks the spacious qualities of the more open landscape of the countryside.

The next picture is of a town where
the road divides, giving a concentrated
view of the near side of the road and
a more open view of the far side. The
lamppost, road sign and parked car give
you an easy introduction to the street
paraphernalia possible in urban scenes.

Here some building works are taking
place in a city location where the
corrugated fence cutting off the work
site from the road reveals the blank
side of a row of buildings, up against
which the new buildings will rise. The
cranes and scaffolding in the centre of
the scene are framed by the large new
buildings on either side.

Seeing Beyond the Mundane

When artists look at buildings, they don't necessarily class them as 'good' or 'bad' or 'pretty' or 'ugly' architecture, but see them as opportunities to produce skilled pictures.

Here, I have taken as my subject the sides of several buildings backing on to a parking lot. They are all parts of the buildings that usually go unnoticed and that very few people would normally want to draw. But to my mind, they seem to take on almost monumental size and power when seen properly. Using a watercolour technique, with one large and one smaller brush, I laid in large areas of flat tone and gradually built up the texture on top of them. You cannot rush this, because you have to wait until one area has dried before you work more detail into it. It helps if, first of all, you outline the main buildings very lightly with pencil. This is a great exercise in keeping control of your medium. Laying down the tonal washes needs considerable concentration to avoid them becoming smudged.

This drawing is after a painting by Charles Ginner (1878–1952) of the River Aire in Leeds, made in 1914. A view of industrial buildings might not at first seem like an attractive subject for an artist, but Ginner used the densely packed forms to create a rich composition, contrasting the red brick walls with blue slate roofs.

A Trip to the City

I decided to go on a journey to find some examples of urban landscapes that had some direct significance for me, so I took the train to London's Trafalgar Square. This is one of the city's main focal points, and I thought that I would be able to find plenty of scenes that gave a good idea of the problems to be solved when drawing in a busy urban environment.

Immediately on emerging from the station I was confronted by two views of the end of a large thoroughfare called The Strand. Here is the mass of lampposts, traffic lights, rubbish bins, bus stops and railings that make up the everyday look of a London street. Notice how the traffic lights and lamp-posts are all clustered together from the position in which I was viewing the scene. I have purposely left the buildings only outlined in order to point out how much of the scene can be taken up with street furniture.

In this picture you can see how the traffic jams in large towns always give a crowded look to the streets and with the lamps and other paraphernalia the whole picture can look very busy. This isn't a bad thing, because this may well be what you want to portray as typical city life.

You can also find big spaces in cities, especially if, as in London, there's a river running through the centre. This view is on the south bank of the River Thames looking up at Waterloo Bridge. There are walkways along the side of the river which allow you to step back and view spaces of path, sky and water, contrasting with the solid architecture of the massive spans of the bridge. The deep shadows under the bridge bring a certain drama to the scene.

This drawing of a pedestrian walkway between shops and restaurants gives a good idea of the bright streets at night in a town. Figures walking along the street tend to look like silhouettes.

Here's a similar effect by daylight, seen from the top of the steps up to the National Gallery in Trafalgar Square. A large ornamental lamp stands in the centre of the picture, and around it can be seen a street of large classical buildings stretching off into the distance. The people dotted about help to define the space between the viewer and the buildings.

And now the view is from the lower part of Trafalgar Square, where the street furniture becomes a way of defining the space between the viewer and the figures and traffic. It's quite difficult to draw people as they pass by in the street, so the best way is to take photographs that incorporate the pedestrians so that you can place them in the scene afterwards. I have used ink here because I find it is sympathetic to drawing the details of the buildings.

A City Panorama

To make a sufficiently dramatic scene to show the most effective method of drawing in the city, I chose as large a panorama as I could of Trafalgar Square, without trying to get everything in.

I placed myself in the middle of the steps of the National Gallery and looked straight across the square towards Whitehall with Nelson's Column right in the middle of the scene, but without being able to see the top, where Nelson's statue stands. This gave me a focal point for the scene without including a large expanse of sky. After all, I wanted to portray the city buildings rather than just the central column.

Step 1

To start with I sketched in the main areas of the blocks of architecture, indicating the open space of the square where people were wandering about. I did this in pencil so that if any of the spaces were wrong I could erase them.

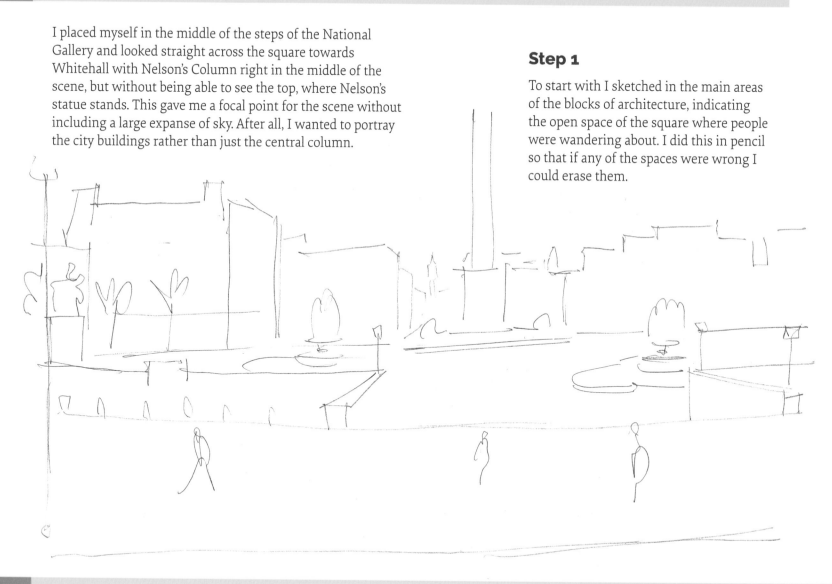

Step 2

Next, still using pencil, I drew up the whole square in some detail, although the large numbers of windows visible were put in as simply as possible. At this stage I could still alter anything that didn't work, and if I decided I didn't like the position of a tree or lamp-post, or even a rooftop, I could get rid of them. My aim was to maintain the overall spacious quality of the scene rather than worry about every detail.

Step 3

Having got the whole scene drawn in I could now put in more people, and add some tone as well. I decided to mainly use ink and so the first thing was to draw the whole picture all over again with a pen. This may seem a bit tiresome, but it can often lead to a better picture. I also started to mark in the tones of the main buildings with a very soft all-over tone, which helped to show up the white splash of the fountains in the square. I did this with pencil to keep it soft at first, then I went over all the areas that I wanted to be more definite with inked-in areas of tone, which looks a lot darker than the pencil. At this stage I put in a lot of people crossing the square and looking at the fountains.

Step 4

Finally, I strengthened parts of the buildings and figures that I wanted to be more obvious, such as the edges of the nearest structures and some of the foreground people. From here on I could add more tone bit by bit with either pencil or ink until I was quite sure that I had given the tonal values their due and made the buildings look as solid as they should. I particularly made sure that the white water of the fountains stood out against darker backgrounds. As in any landscape, the elements further away – in this case the buildings – are less defined than those closer to the foreground.

Using Perspective

As we saw in Chapter 5 (see pages 120–4) perspective is particularly useful for indicating depth of space in an urban environment. These examples show very different views, but all of them are full of man-made features that recede into the distance to give a sense of three-dimensional space.

A classic image of perspective is instantly shown in this drawing of railway lines. The drama of the curve as the rails sweep around to the left where they merge and disappear takes us into the picture and shows us the clarity of perception of the viewer. All that we see beyond the rails are softly silhouetted buildings about half a kilometre away.

The chaos of signs and telephone wires along a Melbourne street give us a sense of the texture of Australian city life. The sweep of the road and the diminishing sizes of the vehicles certainly convince us of the distance observed, and yet the signs and posts flatten out the depth, making it difficult to judge distances.

This drawing of the entrance to the mountain town of Boveglio in Tuscany gives many clues to our position and that of the buildings in front of us. The angle of the steps upwards and the change in size of the windows provide information that helps us to detect how the path winds up into the old town.

Here is a street scene after Hiroshige (1797–1858), the Japanese master of the woodcut, where he depicts a very ordinary Japanese street that has no remarkable architectural features, rather like any suburban high street or a plain terraced street in a medium-sized town. I have eliminated all the figures of passing people in order to show an absolutely simple view of the street where the perspective construction is very evident. The full moon and lit-up windows lend atmosphere to the scene, though I am sure Hiroshige could have created just as brilliant a piece of art with any suburban road at midday. This example was done in coloured pencil and a few lines of ink.

A Scene in Perspective

This is essentially a perspective exercise, applied to an urban scene of your choice. Your eyes will give you all the information you need to draw accurately, but your perspective studies will help the mind to make more sense of it and ease the process of drawing. Choose a location that is easy for you to draw and check on the weather before you start to ensure that rain or wind won't make things more difficult for you.

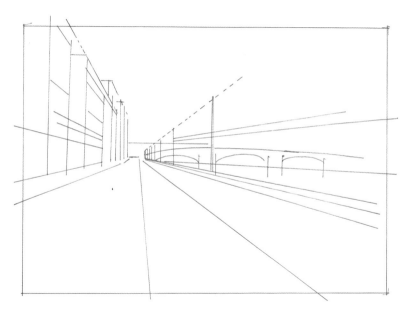

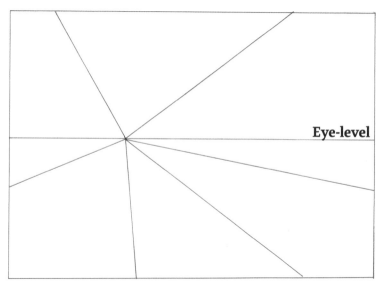

Eye-level

Here is an outline drawing of a street by the Arno river in Florence, Italy. I haven't included any human figures or cars to make it easier to see the perspective.

Now look at this diagram of the perspective lines that underlie the original drawing, consisting merely of the horizon line and the main lines that join at the vanishing point. These should inform your own drawing, even if you don't actually put them all in with a ruler. So your task is to find a street scene and, if it looks too complex, simplify it by leaving out any street furniture and buildings that confuse you. Draw from life, at the scene, bearing in mind what you now know about perspective construction.

Step 1

Put in the main shapes first and the details later, when you are sure that the main blocks of the scene are reasonably convincing.

Step 2

When you have added all the detail you need, put in the tonal areas, using textures to differentiate the various surfaces of the scene. I have given the roadway a smoother texture than elsewhere by smudging the pencil marks with a stump. Notice also how the more distant features have less definition than those in the foreground, which helps to convince the eye of the picture's three-dimensional quality.

Analysing Perspective

In some scenes the perspective construction is less evident but nonetheless important for making sense of the layout of buildings and conveying it accurately. Here we look at a townscape after Walter Sickert (1860–1942) showing a junction where a street divides.

The diagram shows the underlying structure of the scene, which is defined by the perspective of the street winding away on the left and the foreground shopfront at the right edge – thus, two perspective depths which work to the left and right of the picture.

Step 1

Using the diagram as a guide, add the main shapes of the buildings and the road layout. The facade of the central building is relatively detailed and the windows are seen flat on, whereas all of the other buildings, windows and awnings recede from view at a steep angle. Mark in the pedestrians dotted around the scene using simplified forms.

Step 2

When you come to look at the tonal values you can see how the dark cast shadow of the buildings to the right divides the big open space of the foreground street diagonally. It all helps to draw the eye into the centre of the picture and then on down into the far street.

Styles of Architecture

Most buildings are rectilinear, cuboid or cylindrical and do not have ambiguous curves. The challenge of making a structure that remains upright and lasts in time means that the edges of its surfaces are more sharply defined and the shapes much simpler than those found in the natural world. However, architectural styles evolve over time and in many of our urban environments you can find buildings hundreds of years old, juxtaposed with modern-day edifices. The sheer variety of our built environment, especially urban centres, will give you plenty to observe and draw.

Aesthetic and social requirements for living change over time and these can bring about great differences in 'look'. This medieval home (left) was functional for its time, but does not share the sharp, clean-cut lines of its modern counterpart (below).

Here we have two examples of drawings of buildings in which the aim is to communicate something of their materiality and form. The first, of a tower by Christopher Wren, follows the shapes almost as if the artist is constructing the building anew as his pencil describes it.

The approach taken for a famous London landmark, Battersea Power Station, is very different, as befits a great monument to an industrial age.

A very powerful three-dimensional effect has been achieved here by vividly portraying the massive simplicity of the building's design with sharply drawn shadows and large light areas.

This drawing captures the elegant balancing forms of classical architecture as practised by Christopher Wren, with spaces through the form and much articulation of the surfaces to create a lightness in the stone structure as well as visual interest.

Composition and Techniques

Your choice of composition and materials can transform an urban sketch into an interesting artwork. These examples emphasize two different things – one the use of a large mass of details in close-up to make a rich, decorative composition, and the other applying mixed-media to create an airy view of an elegant town square.

This composition is of architecture and trees in Eccleston Square in London. To create it, I started by placing on the left-hand side of the picture a piece of paper that was cut out on the inner side and torn on the outer. I stuck this down with paper glue so that I could work on top of it.

Using a conté pencil, I drew in all the main lines of the windows, trees and railings. Then I went over all the details of the buildings in pen and ink, some parts quite sketchily and other parts more well-defined.

With the conté pencil I marked in the large trees and vegetation, and some of the tones on the collage. Then, with a brush, I washed in the larger shadows on all the buildings and over the conté scribble of the trees and other vegetation. I used two tones of watercolour wash to achieve an effect of depth.

This drawing shows a close-up view of an ornate Russian Orthodox cathedral. It is a composite mass of decorative domes, towers, arches and doorways that seem to have been assembled almost indiscriminately. There is undoubtedly an architectural logic to the whole thing, but from our viewpoint we can't see this. What we can see is detail crowded upon detail, with just a bit of sky at the top to give us an idea of the architectural mass. The picture makes its point by being rich in detail and pushed up against our view so that it almost overwhelms us.

Monet's Gare Saint-Lazare

Monet's famous painting of the huge interior of the Gare Saint-Lazare in Paris uses an Impressionist technique to convey a bustling urban space. The geometric structure of the roof and the buildings in the background are just visible through the haze of smoke rising from the steam engines.

Step 2

Block in the main areas of colour using your pastels and then begin to blend them using the end of your finger or a stump. In some places you may want to overlay two colours and lightly blend them.

Step 1

Pastels are ideal to recreate Monet's scene, as they can be smudged to create an Impressionistic feel. First, spend some time lightly outlining the main shapes of the composition. Pay attention to the lines of the platforms and railway tracks that recede into the distance as these give the composition its perspective depth.

Step 3

Work over the whole picture slowly, filling in any gaps and adding layers of colour. The trick is to overlay colours by lightly hatching or smudging the second colour over the first, but take care not to overdo it or the final effect will be murky. Although the scene is light and airy, there are a few touches of darker shadow around the steam engine, the figures on the platforms and the structure of the station.

Index